YOU ARE THE ARCHITECT OF YOUR LIFE

12 Proven Strategies to Unleash Your Full Potential and Go from Average to High Achiever

ETIENNE H. DJOTO

You Are the Architect of Your Life © Copyright <<2024>> Etienne H. Djoto

All rights reserved. No part of this publication may be reproduced, distributed or transmitted in any form or by any means, including photocopying, recording, or other electronic or mechanical methods, without the prior written permission of the publisher, except in the case of brief quotations embodied in critical reviews and certain other noncommercial uses permitted by copyright law.

Although the author and publisher have made every effort to ensure that the information in this book was correct at press time, the author and publisher do not assume and hereby disclaim any liability to any party for any loss, damage, or disruption caused by errors or omissions, whether such errors or omissions result from negligence, accident, or any other cause.

Adherence to all applicable laws and regulations, including international, federal, state and local governing professional licensing, business practices, advertising, and all other aspects of doing business in the US, Canada or any other jurisdiction is the sole responsibility of the reader and consumer.

Neither the author nor the publisher assumes any responsibility or liability whatsoever on behalf of the consumer or reader of this material. Any perceived slight of any individual or organization is purely unintentional.

The resources in this book are provided for informational purposes only and should not be used to replace the specialized training and professional judgment of a health care or mental health care professional.

Neither the author nor the publisher can be held responsible for the use of the information provided within this book. Please always consult a trained professional before making any decision regarding treatment of yourself or others.

For more information, email youremailhere@youremail.com.

ISBN: 978-1-0698948-3-0 - Hardcover
ISBN: 979-8-89694-128-6 - eBook

My daughters (Serena and Nathalie Djoto)
Thank you for asking me about my work and how I progressed daily. I love you more than words can express. You are my light and my daily motivation.

Contents

Preface xi
Introduction 1

Chapter 1: Your Clarity: Your *Why* 5
Chapter 2: Goal Setting 13
Chapter 3: Improve: Measure and Optimize Your Time
            Management 20
Chapter 4: Personal Development 30
Chapter 5: Work on Your Fitness and Well-being 35
Chapter 6: Develop Your Leadership Skills 42
Chapter 7: Develop Your Communication and Listening Skills 48
Chapter 8: Develop Your Selling Skills 55
Chapter 9: Attract, Make, Save, and Invest More Money 61
Chapter 10: Habits and Routines 80
Chapter 11: The Power of Your Choices 94
Chapter 12: Eliminate Fear and Procrastination 100

Conclusion 108
Acknowledgments 111
Appendix 113
ABOUT THE AUTHOR 117

DOWNLOAD YOUR FREE ULTIMATE PRODUCTIVITY PLAYBOOK & TAKE CONTROL OF YOUR LIFE!

READ THIS FIRST

Thank you for investing in You Are the Architect of Your Life! To help you take action and see real results, I'm giving you The Ultimate Productivity Playbook—completely FREE! Inside, you'll discover battle-tested strategies used by top achievers to:

- ✓ Eliminate distractions & stay laser-focused on what truly matters
- ✓ Crush procrastination & take massive action effortlessly
- ✓ Achieve more—without burnout! Learn how to work smarter, not harder
- ✓ Master time management & create unstoppable momentum
- ✓ Boost efficiency with smart habits & daily success rituals
- ✓ And much more…

This is your blueprint for designing a high-performance life!

Don't wait—unlock your full potential now! 👇 Download your FREE copy today! 👇

subscribepage.io/ED_YATAOYL

"Whenever you find yourself on the side of the majority, it is time to pause and reflect."
Mark Twain

Preface

*"The need for change bulldozed a road
down the center of my mind."*
Maya Angelou

Before embarking on my transformation journey, I lived my life following the principles laid down by society. I was consistently doing the wrong things for my future; watching too much television, not reading books, not saving money, and eating junk food instead of making healthy meals. I allowed bad habits regarding my personal development, health, and finances to guide me. I was not courageous enough to make decisions without seeking other people's approval, and I couldn't move forward until someone else agreed or concurred with my approach. I did not understand that what you do consistently can significantly impact your future.

Thinking back, I was looking for someone to blame in case my actions led to bad outcomes. What a shame! In a word, I followed the crowd, and I thought that my ending somehow would be better than anyone else's around me; someone would be by my side to save me when I got older, to take care of me and help me through my elderly years. I was dead wrong.

I have a couple of questions for you:

- Are you happy with what you have and what you have achieved so far in your life?

- Are you stuck living the same way each year, again and again, and calling it a life? Do you want to live the same life until the end of your life?
- Does your life have a purpose? Are you happy with your career path?
- Are you following the crowd and trying to look fabulous in a society where many people are disconnected, checked out, and busy doing stuff that does not matter at the end of the day?
- Are you happy with your bank account? Or are you still living paycheck to paycheck and feeling anxious daily because you can't allow yourself to lose your job?
- Are you on your path to meet your goals this year? Do you know that list of goals you had at the end of last year? Do you remember those goals?
- Are you learning new skills? A new foreign language?
- Are you working out daily to get your health to the next level?

Do the above questions sound familiar to you? If so, you are not alone; I felt the same way a couple of years ago until I participated in an end-of-semester meeting at my former company, where the leadership presented the semestrial company performance results. I was sitting in this big conference hotel room that had been rented for the occasion.

It was not the first time I had attended this meeting, but each time I felt just as nervous, uncomfortable, and out of place when I saw the top management and leadership team getting ready to take on the stage to display their results on the big screen. I think my nervousness was because I felt inferior to them or less intelligent than them, as I believed they had something I did not have.

As I was listening to the CEO, VPs, and senior directors that were one by one presenting their respective results, I started asking myself why I was sitting here and listening to them. Why was I not on stage? Why was I not part of them? What can I do to become one of them?

After nearly four hours of this meeting, I headed back to my office, and on my way back, I kept asking myself the following questions:
- What do all these people have that I do not have?
- How did they get there?
- How can I become one of them?
- What can I start doing right now to get there?
- Where do I start?
- What skills should I learn to become one of them?
- How do I become motivated to reach that level?
- How can I become excellent at everything I do (professionally speaking as well as personally)?
- And so on…

I do not know you directly, and I do not know what your trigger point might be. For me, this meeting was the trigger point for gaining the courage to ask the above questions and seek answers. During my research, I came across people who told me their trigger points were during COVID; some of them said it was when they lost their day job or had their first child.

No matter what your trigger point might look like, please understand no one will do the work for you. Your future and well-being are all on you and no one else. Everything is on you.

The good news?

You have everything you need to change your life completely. The ideas, strategies, and techniques on the pages ahead will give you the blueprint to go from "totally average" to "high achiever" and save you time, hassle, and hard work along the way.

I hope this book will help you find the solutions you seek to get you from where you are to where you want to be five, ten, or twenty years from now. Time is flying by fast, but you can still decide today is the moment to take the time needed to write down your goals, make the necessary changes, go for it, crush it, and work hard to achieve it.

This is only possible if you take action now, which can change your life's direction forever. If you do it, I guarantee your future self will forever thank you for starting today.

In my case, I started my transformation process in my mid-thirties. I wish I could have started sooner, but wishing, willing, and hoping is not applicable if we are serious about working to become the best version of ourselves. It is never too late to start.

In the upcoming chapters, I'll share how I have used those steps to transform myself from an average individual to a high achiever. I'll provide you with a straightforward, step-by-step process. If you commit to it, you'll experience significant success in every area of your life.

Before we start, know that nothing will happen if nothing changes. If you read this book and apply what you learn in the following chapters, everything will change for you. But if you change nothing, I can guarantee that you will still be in the same place next year.

This book is not for everyone; this is not a quick trick for people who dream of becoming successful overnight. This book is for those willing to work hard, thoughtfully, and consistently no matter what life throws at them; they will stay focused and disciplined to reach their goals. If you know you are meant for more than what you have right now, then you are in the right place; stick with me, and let's get started!

My Story

> *"There's always room for a story that can transport people to another place."*
> **J.K. Rowling**

Before I dig in and share what I have done to change my life, I thought it would be interesting to give you a bit of my own story.

For people who don't know me yet, I was born in Cameroon in a city called Douala. I can say that I was very lucky to grow up in a place where my father had a good job; he worked as a director in one of the most incredible companies of this time in Cameroon. My mother was an elementary school teacher. She worked for a few years as a nursing assistant, but her call to educate and help kids at a very young age was so strong she decided to focus exclusively on teaching.

Guess what? Her decision to work full-time as a teacher coincided with when I was starting first grade, so I had my mother as a teacher, and it remains one of my best experiences. She also taught me in third grade (lucky me). My parents worked very hard every day, and I remember that to continue supporting our family, my mother started two side businesses where she cooked and sold food. The money she made selling food was used to buy women's accessories like bags and shoes, which she would then sell for a small profit.

My first job was as a PLC (Programmable Logic Controller) developer. After a couple of years, I changed career paths and began working as a testing engineer in a big rail industry company. It turned out this company was a Canadian company, which meant I had to move. After being relocated to Toronto for over a full year, I went to Germany, where my next assignment was for a project in Switzerland.

During this time, my former colleagues in Toronto (Ontario) and Saint-Bruno (Québec) asked if I was interested in returning to Canada by an internal transfer. After discussing it with my wife, we decided to move back to Canada.

It was not an easy choice; we knew we would be leaving friends and family behind. Because we had already spent over a year in Toronto, we decided to return to enjoy an excellent quality of life, learn about a new culture, and improve our English.

During all this time, I was working as an engineer. I was making what society will call "good money," but I could not see how we could have a great life if I continued doing what I was doing. As Robert

Kiyosaki said in *Rich Dad Poor Dad*, "I did all that society expected me to do, meaning I went to school, got good grades, got married, had kids, and bought a house."

So, why did my life still feel so unstable? Why did it seem like I couldn't see the end of the horizon? What did I do wrong? I followed what one of my mentors, Robin Sharma (more on him later and the impact he had on my life), called the PANEM (Parent Association News Environment Media). I followed all their advice and was still wondering why I kept living paycheck to paycheck.

It's surprisingly simple. I was not taking myself seriously.

I often complained about my company not paying me well or blamed the tax system or the government for my troubles. It was everyone's fault but *mine*. When I understood that all was on me and no one was going to do the work for me, my life shifted for the better. I took full responsibility and started saving money. I put aside 10 percent of my paycheck, cutting unnecessary expenses. And anytime I had a tax return, I saved all of it.

Finally, after five years of hard work and constant saving, we bought our first house in a small city in Québec. I couldn't see how our future could change after spending all our savings on the house. Yet, I kept repeating the cycle—working hard, saving, and hoping for a better future.

Year after year, I kept getting a 3 to 5 percent raise but didn't seem to see how my future could be better. The slight raise (sometimes just above inflation) was insufficient to keep saving money using the system I had originally put in place. Deep inside, I knew life had more to offer in terms of fulfillment and abundance. But I also knew that to find fulfillment and abundance, I needed to change what I was doing. Otherwise, I was never going to see different results.

One year later, we had our second daughter. My wife had to stay home for one year, and guess what, all the savings we put aside almost disappeared during this time.

As stated, I got a call to take care of my life that day, and I started asking all these questions about them and not me. I decided to take back the overall control of my life, as I also realized that no one would come to save me, that I'm the architect of my life and it is only if I decide to change that everything else will change for a great future. I came from an ordinary family from Cameroon. If I can do it, you can do it too.

Let's dive into my transformation process, where I'll share with you the twelve practical strategies I learned during my journey and all the virtual mentors I had that helped me become the best version of myself. Fasten your seat belt, and let's start.

Introduction

"The journey of a thousand miles begins with one step."
Lao Tzu

It was a Saturday evening, and I was at my brother's house in Laval with one of my childhood friends. We were in the basement, enjoying the evening together. My brother showed us a book with the title *Training Camp* by Jon Gordon and told us everyone in their company had been asked to read it and reflect on it. I wasn't much of a big fan of reading books, but I took a picture of the book, and on my way home, I decided to order the book on Amazon.

This book was filled with strategies and techniques anyone could apply, and if applied consistently, could get big results. In this book, Jon Gordon referred to other books, and I was so consumed by the ideas he shared, I decided to also order all the books he referred to. This is how I became a reader, and since then, I have never left the house without a great book.

This book was the beginning of every change in my life. Jon Gordon's book led me to read other books that helped me develop the strategies and techniques I'm about to share with you.

No one is born smarter, better, or more talented than you. All skills are learnable. If you decide to put in the effort and work hard, you will be able to master any skill, from leadership to finances, information technology, coding, learning a new language—or anything else that might catch your eye!

Based on my experiences this past year, I have learned new skills in leadership and sales, improved my communication skills, and vastly improved my English. At the same time, I have been trying to keep my German at a very high level. In October, I started learning Portuguese. If I can do that, you can do it too, and it doesn't matter how bad you are in a particular skill; the room for improvement is *limitless*.

The first thing you need to do is take a hard look at your life and do a self-assessment of where you are right now and where you want to be five, ten, and twenty years from now. Be honest with yourself. Recognize where you are. You need to go through these steps to close the gap between where you are and where you want to be. This is what I call *self-awareness*. This self-awareness is the beginning of any transformation in terms of your personal development, time management, family goals, financial goals, fitness goals, and career development.

Once you know your weaknesses, let's say you want to improve your communication or your sales skills, plan and go all in to master that new skill. Work two or three times harder and stay consistent until you master that new skill. I can tell you that if you do that, you will close the gap with your competition.

All the strategies I share in this book will only help if you do the work every single day. You have to work hard, and consistently, every single day with no excuses. Please, remember success takes time; don't start working on improving your communication skills and expect to become a great communicator after two weeks. Don't quit after three weeks. It doesn't work like that.

Instead, fall in love with the process of getting better every day. Don't look at the outcome; keep progressing and growing daily, and the outcome will manifest itself automatically. Don't quit after two weeks of trying; stay in the game and trust the process and your plan. Keep pushing and stay consistent, and your future self will thank you.

I believe everything worthwhile in life starts with clarity, vision, and a strong reason, so let's move to the first strategy that will set you up for success.

Chapter 1

Your Clarity: Your *Why*

Your Clarity

"It doesn't matter where you are coming from.
All that matters is where you are going."
Brian Tracy

Having a vision and clarity in your life can be the stepping stone that will put you on the path to success. Unfortunately, most people do not have a clear vision for their life. This is the reason why most of the time people just follow others on social media, get stuck in a job that they hate, have no financial plan, no family plan, no fitness well-being plan, and the list goes on.

I was there for a long time until I committed to taking control of my life and decided to work hard to become the best version of myself. I did not have any clear vision and direction on where I wanted to go, I had no financial plan, and I didn't save money regularly. In a nutshell, I had no long-term vision for myself, and I knew deep inside me that things needed to change. But before going deeper, let me ask you these ten questions:

- What does your life look like right now?
- What goals have you accomplished in the last year, quarter, or month?
- What progress have you made so far in terms of learning new skills?
- Who have you become? Is the person you are today the person you want to become?
- Do you want the next three months to be different from the three previous ones?
- Would you like this year to be different from last year? Are you willing to pay the price and work hard, hard, hard to get there? Or will you find excuses and miss the opportunity to become the best version of yourself?
- Do you know precisely what you want, and what you do not want, out of your life?
- Are you proud of what you have gotten so far? Are you proud of what you have right now in each area of your life?
- Do you have a clear vision you want to work toward? Let's discuss this for the next five, ten, and twenty years.
- Do you know your current destination? Where do you want to go? Which path are you on right now?

Now, take fifteen minutes and write down a clear answer to each question. Be serious and write it down.

Welcome back!

Get this: You can make excuses for the circumstances of your life, or you can decide to take back control and have a clear vision of where you want to be in the future. This is the starting point that everyone should know before going through personal transformation. These are the questions everyone should ask themselves and be honest when providing answers. Be honest with yourself, write your answers on paper, and have a hard look at where you are right now.

Every question mentioned above should give you the awareness to know exactly where you are in your life right now. I want to remind you that we all have the same twenty-four hours, and the question to answer is why some people can achieve more—write books, be serial entrepreneurs, have a great family life, be physically fit—and have more money than the vast majority of the population. The answer is quite simple; it is because they understand the power of having a clear vision and they know exactly what they want out of life. Their clarity gives them the direction they need to take every single day in terms of focus, personal development, fulfillment, skills, and the like.

My lack of vision and clarity made me feel overwhelmed, stressed, and anxious most of the time because I could not get my projects done on time, didn't have enough money saved, and procrastinated on my most important activities regularly. Why did I do that? Because I didn't have a crystal-clear destination for where I wanted to go in my life.

Knowing that the first step to taking control of your life is to get serious by being aware of exactly where you want to go, making a plan, and taking daily actions to get there, I decided to go all in and apply this strategy for myself. I started reading every book I could get my hands on and listening to audio programs on that subject. Going through this exercise, I learned a few things that successful people do regularly once they are crystal clear on their vision and have identified where they want to go:

- They say no to everything that is not aligned with their vision and goals.
- They use their time wisely, efficiently, and better than anyone else.
- They use their phone as a servant instead of playing games, chitchatting, and scrolling all day long.
- They refuse to go out or hang around just for the sake of hanging around, and use this time to read, rest, reflect, and spend time with their family.

- They make sure that every action they take and decision they make is aligned with where they want to go, and where they want to be five, ten, or twenty years from now.

When you have a clear vision for yourself and where you want to be in the next few years, you will automatically stop wasting your time and remove all distractions from your life. You will invest your time wisely, and you will only work with people who inspire, motivate, and appreciate you. You will stop spending your time with people who don't help you grow. You will remove all the people who drain your energy from your life. You will shift your mind from being a victim and complaining all the time to becoming the hero of your life, a high achiever, a doer, a believer, and so on. You will start your day with your most important and difficult task and will eliminate and remove procrastination from your life.

Once you develop a strong vision for yourself, everything around you will change as you become more aware of your time. You will make sure every hour is aligned to bring you closer to where you want to go. Going through this difficult but necessary exercise will help you become crystal clear about where you want to go. This will remove all the roadblocks that were keeping you busy with the things that matter less. Every action you will take and every decision you will make will be directly linked with your biggest vision.

Your *Why*

> *"If the WHY is powerful, the HOW is easy."*
> **Jim Rohn**

Once you are crystal clear on where you are and where you want to go in life, the next step will be to look deep inside you and find your *why*. This step was one of my turning points. Having a clear purpose for what you want and a clear sense of direction will help you identify what you want in life. This step is one of the most important for everyone who is looking to change their life and take the path to success. You have to have a burning desire to let go of the person you are today to become the person you are meant to be. Finding your *why* is key to keeping your clarity alive, and I guarantee you that this is one of the most important and difficult questions to ask and to answer. A strong *why* is what makes your vision, and your clarity, real and will keep you motivated throughout your journey when things become tough or when you lose motivation.

I know how hard it can be to find your *why* in life. We are so overwhelmed today that we live a life without purpose, and we follow the crowd. In this first step of our journey together, I would like to share with you the questions you should ask yourself that will help you find your *why*.

Let's be clear, finding your *why* will take some time, and you will have to have a very difficult, but necessary, discussion with yourself to do it. But once you find your *why*, this will become a fuel to help you start your transformation and stay in the process long enough to see results, especially when you need a lot of motivation and discipline to keep going.

How did I find my *why*? It took me weeks, even months, to find it. I read books, listened to podcasts, followed experts, took a lot of long walks, questioned my life, had difficult conversations with myself trying to understand who I am and how I want my daughters, family, and close friends to remember me. Finally, I came up with a couple of questions that may also help you find your *why*. I guess what I'm suggesting to you is this: Your *why* is the beginning of your journey if you take the time to find it.

Before we start, take the time to think about your big five to ten life goals that you would like to achieve. At least one of them should be much bigger and greater than yourself. For example, as a top professional soccer player, I want to stay in great shape and see my grandchildren grow up. It could be something like wanting to be incredibly good at your craft and serve your clients well, which will help you earn more money.

This goal should consider at least the following four aspects: your personal development, health, family, and prosperity.

1. Why do you want to work on your personal development? What is your passion? What one thing would you love doing without getting paid for a long period and never want to give up no matter what? Furthermore, are you living and enjoying your life (family, craft, passion, fulfillment, etc.), or are you living from paycheck to paycheck (earning a living, hating your day job, not having time for your family, etc.)?
2. Why do you want to be financially free?
3. Why do you want to live your life on your own terms?
4. Why do you want to start your own business/company and become a great entrepreneur?
5. Why do you want to spend quality time with your family? What is your fight? Is your fight greater than yourself? For example, your family and your children.
6. Why do you want to be physically fit?
7. Why do you want to take your life to the next level? Where do you want to be five, ten, fifteen, and twenty years from now? You have the power to become anything you can dream of. You have right now inside you what it takes to accomplish more than you have ever dreamed of in your life.

Once again, I know it is not easy to find your *why*. If it was, everyone would go through this exercise and find it. But I assure you, this is very important if you want to keep going when adversity knocks on your door. If you do not have a strong *why* deep inside you, you will go back to your old self and back to your comfort zone. You will continue to live your life based on other people's opinions, and you will continue to follow the crowd and social media.

Take the time you need to find your *why*, your true *why*. Try to answer the above questions one by one, and I'm sure you will find your ultimate *why*. What is my *why*?

My *why* is as follows:

"I want to live my life on my own terms, making my own choices and decisions, help my lovely daughters become the best versions of themselves, and be physically fit so that I can dance with them at their weddings and see my grandkids grow up."

This is the reason why I wake up early in the morning, why I walk every single day and train three times a week in the gym, why I save and invest more money than ever before, and why I work very hard on my personal development by learning one or two new skills every year. This is the reason I'm building my library at my house, as I know this will be one of the best gifts I will give to my daughters. My *why* is the reason I keep going no matter what challenge or roadblock I face.

Always remember that you're the architect of your life and the creator of your destiny, and no one is going to come to save you. Decide that you are not going to live the same life on repeat. Decide today that other people's opinions should not prevent you from pushing toward your major goal. Your *why* should be strong enough to motivate you long enough into the process.

The main objective here should be to stay in the game longer than anyone else and keep going no matter what challenges and obstacles you encounter. Never, ever let anyone tell you what your strengths are or are not. This is their opinion, and someone's opinion should not separate you from your most important goal in life.

Thomas Carlyle says it elegantly: "A person with a clear purpose will make progress on even the roughest road. A person with no purpose will make no progress on even the smoothest road."

The first steps to success and abundance in life begin with clarity and vision, knowing exactly who you are, what you want, and where you want to go. Never give up, and get serious about it!

Action Steps

- Become crystal clear with your vision of what direction you want to take in your life.
- Commit to having an honest conversation with yourself and discover who you are, what you want, where you want to go, and what your passion is.
- Take the time you need to find your *why* and resolve today to become the best version of yourself.

Finding your *why* will be the key factor to staying motivated even when you face roadblocks, setbacks, and mistakes along your journey.

This first step is so important if you are serious about becoming the best version of yourself and working toward your vision and your goal. Being crystal clear on where you want to go with a strong *why* associated with your goals is crucial for your success. Follow me into the next chapter, and let's see how to set achievable goals.

Check out the Appendix for the list of books that I highly recommend if you want to dig deeper into this subject.

Chapter 2

Goal Setting

*"If people are not laughing at your goals,
your goals are too small."*
Azim Premji

Being crystal clear on your vision is the first step to success. This will give you the awareness to know where you are, what you want, and where you want to go. I think we all agree on that. But let's also be clear that only having clarity with a strong *why* is useless if you do not associate your goals with this vision and clarity—having a strong *why* as well as making a plan to work toward your goal is what will separate you from the rest.

Get this: A dream without a plan is nothing more than a wish. If you want to have success in life, you must decide exactly where you are, who you want to be, and where you want to go in one, five, ten, and twenty years from now. Make a plan, write it down, take action, commit to paying the price, and work hard every day to reach that goal. Make sure to do something every single day that will get you closer to your biggest goal.

I never really had big goals in my life until I decided to take control of them. I was just like the 95 percent of the population who had big dreams inside their heads but never left their comfort zones, continuing to live paycheck to paycheck, and living the same way every year. I was always looking to have other people's approval before doing something. I was afraid to fail, and other people's opinions were deciding my faith and destiny. I couldn't make any decision or follow my dreams without seeking other people's feedback.

Once I got feedback from a family member or closest friend, I felt comfortable with my decision. If you asked me who these people were and why I relied on them, I could not have answered you. I didn't know at that time that when you seek advice, you should only seek it from the people who know how to become the best version of themselves, those who know how to save and invest money, those who know how to work on their personal development, and those who know how to stay fit. I was living in my fears and was seeking advice from people who never followed their own advice.

My life never changed. I was frustrated, not getting anywhere with my life, and just found myself continuing to dream of a better day, month, quarter, and year. But as you already know, if nothing changes, nothing changes.

As Henry Ford says: "If you always do what you've always done, you'll always get what you've always got."

Can someone tell me why the school system does not teach the simple principles of goal setting? We learn a lot of lessons in school, from primary school to college and university, but I really wish that someone had taken the time throughout those years to teach us how to set, optimize, and work toward goals every single day.

Let me be very clear with you. If you decide to only apply one principle of this entire book, I will say take this one, as goal setting is a powerful tool that can help you become the best version of yourself and live the life you were meant to live. But that will only be possible if you do the work. The best-selling author Brian Tracy says it so powerfully: "To unlock and unleash your full potential, you should make a habit of daily goal setting and achieving for the rest of your life."

In other words, write down your goals for the months, quarters, and years to come and work on them daily. If you don't do it, nobody is going to do the work for you; you will keep living the same life without any real progress.

What I can tell you after going through this exercise is that it's no greater satisfaction for me knowing that I am intentionally working on achieving my goal every single day. I'm not saying that it would be easy for you. You will face challenges, fears, and roadblocks, but if you know why you are doing it, you will face it and overcome it.

How to Set Goals and What Questions to Ask Yourself

"If no one thinks your goals are crazy. You are probably not aiming high enough."
Bob Rotella

I decided to go all in and read all of the books I could get my hands on and listen to audiobooks to learn how to set up goals. I realized that I needed to have long-term, mid-term, and short-term goals and that my short-term goals should be aligned with my long-term goals. I decided on:

- Ten-year goal (long-term)
- Five-year goal (mid-term)
- One-year goal (short-term)

Why ten, five, and one?

My ten-year goal is my long-term vision in terms of my craft, health, family, money decisions, travel, and visiting new places with my family.

My five-year goal is more about what I want to achieve five years from now, which is still aligned with my ten-year goal and long-term vision.

My one-year goal drives me to focus daily, helping me achieve personal growth, health, family time, support my daughters' growth, and improve my finances. It aligns with my five-year vision.

Get this: The more you optimize and work hard on your one-year goal, the more you will be on the road to achieving your five-year goals and so on until you get to your ten-year goals. You will have to measure and re-evaluate your goals every month to meet your target. It's time to take a hard look at yourself and ask the following questions:

- What do I need to do for my personal development to become more knowledgeable, add more value, and reach the next level in my domain of expertise?
- What can I do to become fit like a top athlete? What can I do to make this year the best year for my family?
- How much money do I want to make, save, and invest before the end of this year to meet my financial goal?
- Which country/state/place would I like to visit and enjoy?
- Where do I want to live in the next ten years?
- What skills do I need to learn that will help me increase my income?
- What is my financial security number? How much should I save and invest to become financially free?
- And so on...

The next step is to make a list of the goals you want to achieve for the coming twelve months (this is what I call the *month-by-month goal*), five years, and ten years. Make a list for each of these categories, and as stated above, make sure that your twelve-month goals are getting you closer to your five-year goals and so on. While working on your list of goals, make sure that they are:

- **Specific**, meaning if you explain your goal to someone close to you, they will know exactly what you are talking about

without asking too many questions. It should be very clear and easy to understand.
- **Measurable**, meaning make sure that you can track the progress of your goal on a daily or weekly basis and re-evaluate if changes are necessary. Take five minutes at the end of each day, and thirty minutes at the end of each week, and track your progress. Make adjustments where required and keep going.
- **Achievable**, meaning that all your goals can be achieved with your current skill set. If one of your goals requires a new skill, make sure to first add the learning curve of that skill to your list.
- **Relevant**, meaning that you have to make sure that the goal you are working on is aligned with your overall purpose. As stated above, I always make sure that the activities I'm doing regarding my twelve-month goals are relevant to the five-year goals.
- **Time-bound**, meaning each of your goals has a deadline by which you want to accomplish your goal. If you have a big goal, make sure to slice it into small steps and set a deadline for each of the sliced steps until you achieve the biggest one.

These steps have helped me put clarity in all of my goals every year. If you follow them, you will be able to write down your goals, make a plan, and work toward each of them every single day. Without any written goals, I was living with no purpose and objectives. I woke up in the morning with no clear plan on what I would work on first, second, and so on (more on this in the time management section).

Having a clear list of goals brought a lot of purpose and direction to my life. I know exactly what to do from the time I wake up until I go back to bed. I enjoy my days, as I know that every action I take is getting me closer to my five-year goals and, in turn, my ten-year goals.

Action Steps

- Commit today to have one-year, five-year, and ten-year goals. Make sure to have at least the following on your list:
    - Personal development goal
    - Fitness and well-being goal
    - Family goals
    - Financial goals
    - Learning new skills
- Make a list of your goals, write it down, make a plan, take action, and resolve to do something every day toward achieving your biggest goal. Writing things down nearly always promotes greater clarity of thinking. This is why I recommend writing your goals on paper instead of on your phone or tablet. But do what works best for you.
- Use the SMART method when working on the list of your goals. (Specific, Measurable, Achievable, Relevant, and Time-Bound)
- For each goal written on your list:
    - Make a list of everything you can think of to achieve your goals, set priorities for each of them, set deadlines, and take action every day.
    - List any skill you already have or need to acquire that will help you achieve your goals.
    - Identify all the obstacles, difficulties, or roadblocks that can prevent you from achieving your goals or slow you down. Make sure to find solutions to eliminate these obstacles.
    - Track your progression regularly and make adjustments if need be.

While it's crucial to set achievable goals, don't limit yourself, and dare to dream big. Your biggest dream is within reach only if you're willing to put in hard work, determination, and passion.

In other words, grab a sheet of paper, write down everything that pops up in your mind down, and start working on it immediately. Your willingness and determination to take action are what will separate you from average people. Don't be average, and I know you are not average because you are reading this book. Do something every day that moves you toward the achievement of your biggest goal. Consistency is key if you want to succeed in life. With deep desire, determination, and willingness, you already have everything within you to achieve and do big things in life. Don't settle. Your best days are ahead of you. All you need to do is take action and take it now. Goals are not just about what you achieve and accomplish; they are more about who you become in the process of achieving those goals.

In the next chapter, we will explore how you can reach your goals by optimizing your time management and getting more done in a short period of time.

Check out the Appendix for the list of books that I highly recommend if you want to dig deeper into this subject.

Chapter 3

Improve: Measure and Optimize Your Time Management

"The bad news is time flies. The good news is you are the pilot."
Michael Altshuler

Managing and optimizing your time is crucial for your success. Learning to use every hour of your day can be a key indicator of your overall productivity. What separates high achievers is how they plan, use, and manage every hour of their day.

In this chapter, you will learn the simple techniques and methods I have used to change from a poor to a high achiever. If you use it and plan your time well, everything is possible for you. As you can see, after getting crystal clear on where you are in life, the next step is to know how to manage your time efficiently to achieve success in life. You will never have enough time to do all the things you have planned or wanted to do. But you have more than enough time to focus on getting the most important thing done.

I learned that the hard way. For many years, I started my day around 9:00 a.m. and avoided doing my most important tasks. Instead of doing the hard, unpleasant task first, I have always looked for an excuse to put it off. Looking back now, I realized my procrastination was not because I was lazy but because of the negative feeling that was associated with the tasks I had to get done. This, in turn, made me fall behind and probably cost me a good raise and promotion. I used to start my day checking my emails. Anything I had planned to do that day would get pushed aside if I had a high demand from my boss. I would always wait until the last minute to answer emails (luckily, though, most of the time, he didn't need them answered right away).

Does that sound familiar to you? If that is the case, you are not alone. This is because you might not know how to improve your time management. In this chapter, you will learn the simple strategies and techniques that will help you manage your time very well and allow you to get more done in a short period of time and spend more time with the people you love.

To become a high producer, I asked myself the following questions:

- Why can some people write four books a year, take a university degree, manage a team of a hundred-plus people, and travel around the world as keynote speakers, while others cannot?
- Why do some people achieve more, grow daily, do more, and earn more money than others?
- How come they can get so much done in twenty-four hours a day? Are they working around the clock? How do they manage their time?

All these questions made me realize that I needed to change something if I wanted to get more done and enjoy more free time. The difference between high achievers and average people is how they manage and use their time. And how did I do that? I had to apply and use the same strategy that the high achievers do. As you remember from my previous chapter, always learn from the experts.

So, here is what I learned from the high achievers:

- High achievers use their time differently than the average person.
- High achievers start their day with their most important activity and keep doing it until it is completely done before moving to something else.
- High achievers apply the 80/20 rule to everything they do. They know only 20 percent of the things they do count for 80 percent of the results they get. So, they put all their effort into the 20 percent of tasks.
- High achievers use the Eisenhower Matrix. This is a way to organize tasks according to both urgency and importance, helping effectively prioritize your work and set your daily goals. If it is urgent and important, they add it to their list as a top priority and do it immediately. If it is urgent but not important, they delegate. If it is important but not urgent, they schedule it for later. The task will be fully eliminated from the list if it is not urgent or important.
- High achievers use Parkinson's law to accomplish more in less time. They deliberately shorten their schedule and deadlines to achieve more in a shorter period of time. They know that the trap of having a long deadline will lead to procrastination and laziness. So, they will put a little bit of pressure on themselves to get it done fast by applying a state of urgency to each task. Most of the time, high achievers will not take Friday into consideration when planning their week or will stop their workday between 4:00 and 5:00 p.m., so it forces them to focus on what truly matters to get the job done faster than anyone else.

This was eye-opening for me; I realized that highly productive people know that time management skills are essential to be proficient in every area of their lives. Experts in time management understand that working time is working time, so when they work, they do it seriously by staying with their most important task and getting it done before moving to the next task. They don't switch between tasks; they put all their energy and concentration into the task they are working on until it's completely done.

To reach this level of concentration, they create an environment where they can fully focus. This realization made me recall what my former project manager did when we were working on a project. He reserved a room just for our team and called it our "war room."

He reserved this room in another building that was hard to reach, and we spent a couple of hours a day in that room. This was before COVID, and hybrid work was not as popular as it is today. We got much more done when we were in that room. I asked him how he managed his time, and he told me that to get more done, he blocked off a couple of hours in the morning and reserved a room where he could get lost for three to four hours with deep focus and no distractions. He always protected his morning time at all costs and used the afternoon time for meetings or less-urgent tasks.

I know it is not always easy to apply this approach while working in an open space where anyone can pass by and distract you. If you want to increase your productivity, you have no choice but to master your time management. Find a way while you're working to protect at least a couple of hours during the day to increase your productivity and use the afternoon for other activities such as meetings and administrative work. What took me one to two weeks to accomplish in the past now took me four to five hours of intense and focused work. I do the same for the most significant tasks: slice them into mini-tasks and tackle them individually.

Embrace the transformative power of the 80/20 rule and Parkinson's law. These principles, when applied, can revolutionize your approach to time management and productivity, leading to a more efficient and fulfilling life.

> *"We always have time enough, if we will but use it aright."*
> **Johann W. von Goethe**

I have never seen someone master time management with a high level of productivity who does not apply the 80/20 rule, also called the Pareto principle (from Vilfredo Pareto), along with Parkinson's law. These principles have helped me master and optimize my time management, and they are pretty simple but not easy to apply and follow.

One reason why people fall behind is a poor management system; most of the time, they do not realize it. They are too busy doing the wrong thing to notice everyone around them. One thing I want to emphasize that will help you reach the next level is that increasing your productivity is not only for your professional growth and success but also for your life goals and achievements.

The same applies to your personal growth. The world is moving very fast, and we get bombarded daily with so much information and distractions. I keep seeing people around me waste their time in activities that they hate and thus have no motivation, but they keep doing it to be friendly, even when they know those time-wasting activities are not aligned with their overall goals and are preventing them from working on their most important tasks.

Let's now look closely at effective strategies to significantly increase productivity and enhance overall results in both personal and professional goals. By implementing these two principles, you can optimize your time management and efficiency.

80/20 - Pareto Principle

We can easily become overwhelmed with daily tasks and not know where to start. Most of the time, we take the easy way and start with the bottom task of our list. The flip side of doing so leads us to procrastinate on our most important tasks, which, if done correctly, will help us achieve more and progress faster in our careers and lives.

I challenge you to look at how you organize your day and to note what activity you are starting your day with.

If you have a list of ten tasks to accomplish for that day, resist the temptation to start with the easiest one; instead, identify the 10 to 20 percent of activities on that list and start with them. Put the 80 percent for later and don't touch anything on the 80 percent list until you have thoroughly finished the 20 percent activities on your list. This is what the 80/20 rule is. This rule can change your life, business, and career.

I wish I had learned this rule back in school or when I started my career. I'm wondering why this law is not taught at high schools, colleges, and universities. Speaking from my own experience, I was always in a reactive mode, meaning as soon as an email reached my inbox, I jumped in and answered. This led to breaking my focus most of the time, and in the end, I was so frustrated that I chose to do the easy tasks. This made me feel like I was winning in the long term, but it was the opposite. I didn't realize that focusing on the bottom 80 percent of my list of tasks was another form of procrastination, which never helped me.

Here is the deal: No matter how hard you work on the 80 percent tasks of your list, no matter how good you are at that level, you have to understand that it is not the volume and quantity of hours you put in; it is the quality of the work you do very well at the top 20 percent that will separate you from the bottom 80 percent.

Here are some examples to consider going forward:
- Twenty percent of your task will produce 80 percent of your results.
- For entrepreneurs, 20 percent of your customers will account for 80 percent of your revenue.
- Twenty percent of your daily habits and activities will account for 80 percent of your success.

- Twenty percent of your employees will earn 80 percent of your total revenue.

From now on, track and identify the 20 percent of your tasks or activities that will produce 80 percent of your results and let go of the bottom 80 percent that only provide 20 percent. To do so, ask the following questions:
- Am I about to do this activity or task that falls in the 20 percent or the bottom 80 percent?
- Will what I'm doing now produce more results and impact, or am I just busy doing easy stuff?
- Am I using my time on my most important tasks right now, or am I doing things that do not lead me to my goals?

Never start your day without identifying your most critical tasks or activities that will account for 80 percent of your total result.

Parkinson's Law

In today's world, the vast majority of people are working a regular nine-to-five, and the big trap here is to think that you always have at least eight hours to complete your work. Even worse, people are used to bringing work back home and continuing to work until late at night. From my perspective, this harmful habit leads to neglecting your family life and personal well-being.

Does this sound familiar? No worries. I was doing the same, spending eight hours or more in the office and most of the time bringing work back home. I was doing so until I understood Parkinson's law, which completely changed my working method.

This law states that a task would expand in relation to the time allotted to its completion. In other words, if you give yourself two weeks to complete a task, you will think that you have enough time ahead of you and will not do what is necessary right now to complete the task. On the other hand, if you have a short deadline, such as one day, to complete the same task, you will be more focused and do whatever it takes to complete it within that timeframe.

With the example I gave you above, when you think that you have eight hours to complete your work, you will find a way to fill in those hours; if you set aside two hours, you will increase your focus and do it in just two hours, and so on.

This is what I call the magic of a shortened deadline. Can you imagine applying this law to everything you do? No matter what project deadline you have or get from your boss, let's say four weeks, for example, shorten this time to one week and see what happens.

You must always apply these two principles together to increase your productivity. Doing so will make you one of the most productive people you know in every environment.

Effective time management saved my career and my life. I have more time to enjoy and work on other projects, like writing this book. Looking back, this was impossible to accomplish in the past because of my poor time management. Let's dive right into the simple strategies and techniques you can start to implement right now and see the results.

Action Steps

- Prepare your upcoming week by setting aside time on Saturday and/or Sunday to plan out your schedule.
- Hold yourself accountable to your schedule, block your essential tasks in your calendar, and review and adjust your plan for each day the night before (this will help you add or remove tasks from your list based on your priorities).
- Apply the 80/20 rule to everything you do. Not all tasks are equal in terms of consequence. Prioritize your tasks based on their significance and consequence, not their urgency.

- Eliminate and remove all distractions when you work on your most important task. If you work at the office, find your "war room" and get lost there for at least three to four hours. Then, use your morning time to get more done.
- Use Parkinson's law to accomplish more in less time every week until it becomes a habit.
- Avoid multitasking, instead use the Pomodoro technique. Choose a task. Set a twenty-five-minute timer. Work on the task every single morning. Take a short break (ideally five minutes) after the end of twenty-five minutes. Repeat.
- Always start your day with your most important task, focusing on one task at a time. Have one top-priority task for the day. Don't do anything else until you get your top-priority task done.
- Work a chunk of hours, and protect the first hours of your day at all costs.
- Use the afternoon for your less-important tasks like meetings, email, return calls, etc.
- At the end of each day, take five to ten minutes to evaluate your day, look at how you show up during that day and what can be improved for the next day, and do it. Never forget that only what gets measured can be improved. You cannot improve what you don't measure.
- Always work from the list you created the night before. This is your blueprint. Never work on a new task without adding it to your list. Doing so will derail your entire day, cause you to lose momentum, and frustrate you.
- Resist the temptation to check your email and notifications during your blocking time. Check your emails at most two times a day (preferably around noon and 4:00 p.m.). This will help you see if something urgent pops up, and if it does, add it to your list for the next day.

- Become the master of saying, "No." Do this at least once during your most productive time of the day.

Effective time management is the key to maximizing your overall productivity and achieving your biggest goals. In a nutshell, the key to becoming more productive is prioritizing your most important task and getting busy doing it until it gets done. This chapter is closely bound to the previous one. We know that high achievers take a moment each weekend to reflect and identify any area of their time management where they can optimize. They know better than anyone else how important it is to continually monitor and improve their most important asset in life: *time.*

Look at the action steps above and see what suits you best. Then, use at least one of these strategies and see how it goes. Once you master one of those strategies, move on to the next one. Do it until you get comfortable doing it without thinking about it. You will become a high achiever in a relatively short time.

Now that we have identified the techniques that will help us be more productive by using our time well, let's now see how we can use this to work on our personal development.

Check out the Appendix for the list of books that I highly recommend if you want to dig deeper into this subject.

Chapter 4

Personal Development

"Successful people do the things that unsuccessful people are unwilling to do."
John Maxwell

It has never been as easy to become great in your field of expertise as it is today. You can become all you have always dreamed about if you work to get there. Personal education is the key to legendary success, and you can become more knowledgeable than ever for free using YouTube or with a bit of investment by using Udemy, Codecademy, Khan Academy, Google search, and the list goes on. You can decide to learn any subject or skill, and you are only one fingertip away.

We get surrounded daily with notifications, emails, and calls, and we may not find the time to learn and absorb. But if you're very serious about personal development and want to reach the next level, you must find the time. In this chapter, I'll share the actions and tactics you can use to become a lifelong learner, add more value in the marketplace, and dominate your field.

How did I become a lifelong learner?

"Continuous learning is the minimum requirement for success in any field."
Denis Waitley

I wish someone would have told me personal development is the key to success if you want to earn and grow more. I must admit, after I left university with my degree in my pocket, I stopped reading books and learning. I stopped investing in myself. I was like most of the young people of my generation. I went to work, went back home, sat down and watched television, had an after-work party with my colleagues every other week, and repeated it week after week. My salary stayed low and rose with inflation, sometimes slightly less than inflation. At that time, I thought the only way to get a big raise was to change the company; this is at least what I thought. I did it for about ten years until I started asking all these questions.

This is when I finally realized that I was the architect of my own life. No one is going to come and save me, no one owes me anything, and no one will ever pay me good money if the value I put on the table is not high enough.

So, I began researching and reading every book I could get my hands on, and I discovered that successful people, the high achievers, all follow the same recipes. They invest thoughtfully in themselves every single day. They get 1 percent better every day; they don't compare themselves to others; they don't wish and hope; they go all in and put in the work to become the best versions of themselves. High achievers know that knowledge is only power if you apply it well, so they get out and apply what they have learned.

Successful people don't stop here; they measure and optimize their learning process and how they show up daily. As you already know, only what gets measured can be improved. They arrive on time for the meeting or five minutes before the meeting commences. They invest in webinars, online courses, and books.

High achievers apply the 80/20 rule, as stated by Brian Tracy in one of his motivational podcasts: "Twenty percent of salespeople earn 80 percent of the company profit, and the bottom 80 percent earn the 20 percent left." So, successful people invest in themselves to be part of the 20 percent. Once there, they invest even more in themselves to get to 10 percent, and then 5 percent, and so on.

Looking back, I was in the 80 percent, and my habits had nothing to do with what people in the 20 percent did to get where they were. I slept longer hours, woke up late, never read or enjoyed life, and got stuck in the same position. It is very painful for me when I look back. This part of my life was just who I was then. One of the lessons here is that it doesn't matter where you are now. You can change your destiny by applying the same strategies you are about to learn in this chapter. Is this easy to do? Hell no!

If it were, everyone would be doing it. It will require total commitment and focus on developing yourself, growing, and becoming more valuable in the marketplace.

Who do you spend time with?

Jim Rohn said, "You are the average of the five people you spend the most time with." In other words, have a hard look at your inner circle, career, bank account, salary, and how you communicate with others. Are they negative complainers, scrolling all day, finding excuses, and blaming all the time? How do you feel when you are around them? If you feel drained, please find a way to remove all the negative people from your life. They are the ones who drain you all the time, who criticize you, and never support you. Instead, be around people who motivate you, support you, and keep pushing you to go the extra mile.

I'm going to repeat that because I think it's worth saying: *You are the architect of your life.* You may say, "Well, this sounds good, but I feel so overwhelmed that I don't know where to start," and I would say, "Start right now. I guarantee that your future self will thank you for taking this first step today. This will be one of the best decisions of your life." Keep repeating this mantra every morning: *I am committed today to becoming a lifelong learner.* Robin Sharma, the best-selling author of *The 5AM Club*, says it so powerfully: "Your income and impact always reflect your self-identity." My interpretation is that what you get from the marketplace is proportional to your output and value. So, if you want to earn more, learn more, invest more, and read more. As Jim Rohn said so elegantly: "You attract money by the person you become."

To attract more money into your life, you have to become a person of value, bring more to the marketplace, and always go the extra mile, and the market will reward you.

Action Steps

Below are the ten strategies that, if you apply consistently and persistently, will allow you to become one of the most influential people in your industry. Let's dive into it right now:

- Plan a dedicated time daily in your calendar to read and learn.
- Take advantage of the opportunity to ask questions to someone more knowledgeable than you.
- Resolve today to be a sponge, seek expert advice, learn from them, take notes, deconstruct what you have learned, and apply it.
- Resolve today to read thirty to sixty minutes every day. Never end a day without reading. For example, read a book while waiting in line or traveling.
- Listen to audiobooks/podcasts while driving or working out.

- Use YouTube as a servant to develop yourself. Many great knowledge content is free on YouTube; use it to your advantage.
- Use Google as your search engine to find more topics related to your learning progress.
- Attend seminars at least two to three times yearly on the subjects that interest you.
- Udemy, Lynda, and Khan Academy are affordable, and you can find great content to help you learn and develop yourself.
- Use the traveling time by train and plane to read and learn. This is valuable time with almost no distractions.

The one who learns the most will always win; investing in yourself is the best investment you can make. Invest as much as you can in yourself as described above; please note that your personal assets will always be more valuable than any other investment. Be willing to learn how to pay for your education and invest the time to improve your craft. What gets you here will never get you to the next level. The moment you stop learning is the moment you stop growing.

As you know, knowledge is power when you apply it.

Check out the Appendix for the list of books that I highly recommend if you want to dig deeper into this subject.

Chapter 5

Work on Your Fitness and Well-being

> *"Your health account, your bank account, they're the same thing. The more you put in, the more you can take out. Exercise is king and nutrition is queen. Together you have a kingdom."*
> **Jack LaLanne**

It was March 11, 2022, and we were still actively dealing with COVID. It was cold outside, and my friend came to visit us. We were having dinner and enjoying our time together. I suddenly felt unwell, so we had to call the ambulance. At the hospital, the doctor told me I had a high level of cholesterol and my blood pressure was high, and this was why I felt so bad. It was due to my blood pressure going suddenly very high. I'm not very overweight, but when I reflected, I was eating junk food a lot, taking my coffee with sugar, adding salt to my food, and the list goes on. This was the day when I decided to get fit like an athlete and completely change my diet. In this chapter, you will learn all the strategies and techniques I have put in place to become fit like, guess what, *an athlete*.

I sat down and reflected on how I was living my life for the past two years, writing it down in my journal. I wrote down everything: my diet, my sugar and salt consumption, how many times I worked out, what I ordered in restaurants, how many hours I slept at night, how many times I walked outside or in the woods, when was the last time I got my eyes checked, and so on.

Once I was done, I called the doctors to make appointments, and went down my list. It took me approximately two months to meet with the doctors and to get back all the results. Now I knew exactly what to do, and where I needed to improve. I had a plan to follow, and I knew that if I followed the plan, I would reach my target of becoming fit. As a wise person once said: "If nothing gets done, nothing gets done, and if you want to have what you have never had before, you have to become what you have never become before."

Here I was with all my medical examination results, and it was on me to take the lead and go to work. Once again, I asked myself the following questions:

- How do top athletes stay in good shape?
- What does their daily routine look like in terms of workouts?
- What books do they read to monitor and optimize their health?
- How do they passively, and actively, rest?
- What do they do in terms of their well-being?
- What does their diet look like?

With all these questions written in my journal, I went out seeking answers. As usual, I began reading all the books I could find on those topics, listening to podcasts, and watching great documentaries about legendary athletes. My search for information made me realize that I was once again in the bottom 80 percent in terms of doing what is required to be in top shape. I found that the top athletes have an optimized lifestyle. When they work, they work hard, and they do it with a high level of focus and consistency. But they also know that to do your best work, you need to take time to rest and recover. They don't feel guilty when they do not work, as they know that resting is part of the game.

During their down time, they invest in activities that energize them and lift their spirits instead of spending it scrolling on their devices all day long. They carefully plan their days by implementing workout routines that will help them keep the momentum throughout each week, as they know that when you win each week, you win your months, quarters, semesters, and years.

I realized that most of them start their workouts early in the morning so that they can have additional workouts during the day. In his best-selling book, *The 5AM Club,* Robin Sharma shared the benefits of working out first thing in the morning using what he called the 20/20/20 formula in terms of reducing fear, beating stress, increasing your focus, reducing your cortisol, increasing your dopamine, and accelerating your metabolic rate. I have applied it since then, and it works so well for me. I saw a total transformation in my focus, my energy, and my metabolic rate. Was it easy to wake up at 5:00 a.m. the first day? *Hell no!* But I kept up the habits. I applied a simple strategy to wake up fifteen minutes before my usual time and kept increasing it bit by bit, fifteen minutes by fifteen minutes. Today, I increased the time and woke up around 4:30 a.m. to give myself more time for me.

My continued search for information led me to John Ratey's book *Spark,* where he shared the result of one of his studies on how a mix of physical activity (walking, running, aerobic exercises, stretching, etc.) can have a positive influence on mental capacity. I implemented this in my workout routine, went all in, and bought a gym membership to have more workout options.

Eventually, I came across Lewis Howes's podcast *The School of Greatness* with Win Hof's interview. Win Hof was talking about all the benefits of breathing exercises, stretching, push-ups, and cold showers. I also came across the *366 Days to Change Your Brain Every Day* from Daniel Amen's book, where he explains the simple daily practice of strengthening your mind, memory, moods, focus, energy, habits, and relationships.

I committed to applying these tactics one by one and seeing which one suited me, and each time, I measured my progress and wrote about it in my journal. I monitored everything to find the best workout exercise that I could apply every day, week, and month.

As you know by now, the way you craft your days will result in you having a good week, and the weeks will become months, quarters, semesters, and years. I kept consistent throughout each week, and I did not let anything prevent me from doing my workout. During rainy or snowy days, I have to confess that it wasn't easy to go out and do my workout, but I remember what Scott Allan said in his book, *Do the Hard Things First*: "Block in five minutes to start doing it." This means that once you have scheduled something, remind yourself to start doing it for the next five minutes, no matter how difficult the task is or how bad the weather is outside. Even if you stop doing it after five minutes, you can be proud of yourself, as you have started and moved forward. This will give you a sense of immediate accomplishment that will increase over time. This is a small win; you will see significant results if you keep doing it consistently. My experience has shown me that starting to do what you have planned for a short period will keep you going most of the time.

This five-minute strategy helped me so many times to avoid procrastination. After five minutes, you often find the momentum, and you keep going.

My quest to get fit didn't let me stop there with my workout session. I aimed to explore any activity that could help my body be strong and recover quickly. This led me to explore massage therapy and cold showers. I invested in a massage therapist once every two to three weeks because of the benefits of the program, such as quicker recovery between my strong workout, a night of better sleep, improved blood circulation, decreased muscle stiffness, and improved flexibility. Again, it all costs a lot of money, but don't forget, it is never the cost but the return on investment that matters.

I started implementing the one-minute rule at the end of each shower. Here is the thing: Every day, I had to go all in with a cold shower for at least one minute to get all the benefits of a cold shower. I kept increasing this time bit by bit, and as I'm writing this book, I spend about five minutes in a cold shower.

During my morning workout, I did a mix of jump rope and push-ups, followed by ten minutes of meditation, six minutes of breathing exercises, and then reading and learning. I stretched during the day; I downloaded a set of stretching exercises on Google and YouTube. I stretched for five minutes after every sixty minutes of intense work during the first four hours of my work. During this break, I drank a glass of water to keep my body hydrated. I invested in a retractable table for my day's work and spent all my meetings standing. In the gym, I never spent more than fifty minutes on my workout session even though I was doing different sets of weights, push-ups, elliptical, functional strength training, and always ended with stretching.

Well-being – Proper Diet

"Eat healthily, sleep well, breathe deeply, move harmoniously."
Jean-Pierre Barral

During my research to improve my physical fitness and my well-being, and find my proper diet, I came across Shawn Stevenson's book, *Eat Smarter*. Shawn's book is full of strategies that you can use to improve your brain function, lose weight, and reboot your metabolism. After reading Shawn's book, I could make better choices in terms of diet. First, I eliminated sugar, rice, and salt. I started eating many vegetables, fish, fruits, you name it. I eliminated junk food from my diet completely, and I drank more water. It's amazing how fast you can get the results when you work out regularly and add a proper diet. After only three to four months, I started feeling great again and had a lot of energy. I increased my focus, and my energy level helped me complete a lot during the day.

My research next led me to how top athletes work on their mental fitness and overall well-being.

Top athletes meditate, practice gratitude, sleep eight hours a night, nap during the day, and spend time relaxing. They know that their free time is precious and use it wisely on activities that energize them and improve their mental health. This allows their bodies to recover, which, in turn, helps them be more productive the following day.

Once I learned these strategies, I set them up in my daily plan. I started aiming for getting at least seven to eight hours of sleep at night by implementing a great nightly routine. I scheduled a fifteen-minute nap at the beginning of the afternoon. I spent good time in nature, and sometimes I just sat near nature and let my mind wander.

The good news is that when we develop a better awareness of the importance of physical activities, having a proper diet, and recovery, we can reduce the probability of getting terrible diseases. The ultimate goal here is extending your longevity by being serious about your fitness.

Action Steps

Below are actions that you can implement to get your fitness to the next level:

- Plan your workouts every day and write them down in your weekly plan. Make sure that you invest at least sixty minutes every day to your fitness.
- Run, walk (in nature if possible), and bicycle regularly, and while doing so, use this time to listen to an educational audio program.
- Get your gym membership and make sure that the time you spend in the gym is recorded. Go all in. Work very hard and

with the required intensity and focus. As mentioned above, listen to an online course that suits your expertise while working out.
- Do a combination of lifting weights, stretching, and cardio.
- Invest in massage therapy and yoga.
- Aim to sleep at least seven to eight hours per night. If your body requires more, sleep more.
- If you're blessed to work from home, explore napping during your workday. It works so well for me and gives me a second energy boost for the rest of the day.
- Get serious about resting and relaxing, and allow your body to recover. Find a quiet place and get lost for a certain period without distraction. Always make sure to use your free time to take care of yourself.
- Practice meditation every day to calm your mind.
- Practice gratitude every day or every couple of days a week. Be grateful for your journey, your daily wins, and your progress.
- Take time to celebrate every win with your family.
- Eliminate or reduce all kinds of junk food, sugar, and salt from your diet. Your future self will thank you. Instead, add a lot of vegetables to your diet.
- Explore breathing exercises.

To see results, you need to be consistent and follow your plan every single week. Every significant achievement starts with simple steps. I know I have shared a lot in this chapter. Take it one bit at a time, keep pushing forward, believe in yourself, and trust the process. You can have it all, but not all at the same time. Be patient, take the time you need, and try to implement these steps one by one.

Check out the Appendix for the list of books that I highly recommend if you want to dig deeper into this subject.

Chapter 6

Develop Your Leadership Skills

"Surround yourself with people that push you to do better. No drama or negativity. Just higher goals and higher motivation. Good time and positive energy. No jealousy or hate. Simply bringing out the absolute best in each other."
Warren Buffett

During my research, one thing kept coming up. This thing was leadership. I learned that successful people are great leaders; they understand that leadership is a work-in-progress, and they know there is no single path to success you must follow to achieve your goals. In his book *Uncommon Leadership*, Ben Newman depicts the eleven uncommon traits of the great leader; he shares the stories of the most impressive elite performers and high achievers of our time. Reading his book taught me that the high achievers are willing to improve their skills, approaches, and beliefs to follow a high standard and keep the bar high.

They are driven by the deep desire to work on their goals longer than anyone else, and to keep asking questions and learning from the best of the best. They are a student-in-progress, and they keep reinventing themselves and continue growing every day. They know one thing: *To be the best, you must learn from the best.*

This brings me back to the beginning of my career when I wanted to find out who influenced me the most. After reading and absorbing a couple of books and listening to podcasts on leadership, I developed the awareness to identify what it takes to be a great leader. To be a leader, you don't need any fancy title right after your name or any academic degree from the top universities. You can decide to be a leader right now where you are with what you have.

Going back to the story, the leader who influenced me the most had all the characteristics that great leaders have. Below are a couple of points that she mastered as our leader:

- She communicated very clearly and transparently with us. As Jon Gordon said, "Negativity will fill in and grow when there is a void in communication. This void in communication has destroyed so many teams, and I recall so many times a team gets killed just because of it."
- She constantly reminded us that she works for us and not the other way around. She clearly understood that being a leader is to serve others.
- She praised us in public and talked about the challenges we were facing in private. She understood very well that leadership is about creating an environment where we will feel safe to maximize our full potential while helping everyone around us do the same.
- When we had a challenge with a supplier, she always took the lead, made the first phone call, and tried to find a solution.
- She passionately and committedly supported the company culture and drove it down to our level.
- She was always solution-oriented and asked us to spend our time trying to find a solution instead of complaining about something we couldn't change. She said, "Let's all put our positive energy into finding a solution together."

- During our one-on-ones, she clearly explained her expectations and told everyone the end goal and why we were aiming for it.

I could go on and on. I guess what I'm trying to tell you is that each of us has had at least one great leader in the course of our careers. The one who makes you reach the next level and helps you become a leader. This leads me to what Gifford Thomas points out in his book *The Inspirational Leader*, which states that leadership is about people. It's about inspiring people to believe that the impossible is possible and building people to perform at heights they never imagined. It's about positively impacting your community, company, department, employees, and the world.

Since then, I have decided to only work with great leaders; I can no longer do otherwise, and you shouldn't either. Life is too short to spend the best time working for someone who doesn't support you and help you become the best version of yourself.

A couple of years later, I was promoted to team lead. I had the chance to apply all that I had learned from my previous manager and add my own leadership style. I had a small team of four people. I kept reminding myself of what Mahatma Gandhi said so beautifully: "A sign of a good leader is not how many followers you have but how many leaders you create."

It wasn't easy, and I made mistakes. Once, we missed an important delivery, and instead of taking the blame and protecting my teammate, I pushed the blame on my colleague. I couldn't sleep very well that night. I went to my teammate the day after and sincerely apologized for my behavior, and I committed that day to never, ever do it again. My gesture touched my teammate so much that he later confessed he didn't expect me to come back to him and apologize. He told me that it was the first time since the beginning of his career that a team lead or manager ever came to him and apologized for the way they treated him. This experience made me realize that to be a good leader, one of the critical requirements is to be a great communicator. From that day, I also decided to invest in my communication skills.

As you might see by now, leadership separates a great company from the average company. Greg Savage said: "People don't leave companies; they leave leaders. When employees leave, it's not 'the company' they blame. It's not the location, or the team, or the database, or the air conditioning. It's the leadership! When people are valued, it's incredible how their whole aura shines brightly. They feel a sense of importance, which inspires them to produce their very best work."

I challenge you to look back at all the places you have worked in the past. You will be able to identify if that company was a great company with a strong leadership culture or a bad one with a poor leadership culture. In the first case, the company will shine and be very strong in the market; in the second case, you will see a high turnover, people will come and go, and human resources will be much busier recruiting new employees all the time.

In his book *The Power of Positive Leadership*, Jon Gordon outlines the strategies and framework everyone can utilize and implement to become a great leader. This is one of the best books I have read on leadership. Applying these strategies and techniques helped me become the leader I was meant to be. Through my research, I understand that to be a great leader, you have to understand the nature of humans and how they think in the moments of good times and when they struggle and go through stressful situations.

Leadership is also about understanding others' passions, interests, well-being, and family. The moment you realize this, it will give you the tools you need to help them move forward when things go well and keep the momentum, but also help them during their moments of struggle. A great leader understands that being able to help with such precision will only happen when their colleagues, friends, and family members trust them, open their hearts to them, and share their struggles with them.

If you work on your leadership skills daily, you will be amazed at how this will impact every area of your life. Decide today to be a lifelong learner and coachable, and to see everyone you interact with as a mentor or teacher that you can learn from. Never miss an opportunity to learn, ask questions, seek advice, absorb, and apply what you have learned. Don't be afraid to talk to people and ask them what they are reading currently or which educational podcasts they are listening to. If your people need your help, take the time to listen carefully to them without judgement and help them as best as you can. Simon Sinek admirably says: "A mentor is not someone who walks ahead of you to show you how they did it. A mentor walks alongside you to show you what you can do."

Be that mentor and help people you lead also become leaders.

Action Steps

- Identify the people whose leadership styles you admire the most and resolve today to read their books and apply their techniques and strategies. Follow them on social media, and don't hesitate to ask for advice. My leadership models are Jon Gordon, Robin Sharma, Simon Sinek, Gifford Thomas, Dr. Jill M. Siler, and Adam Grant. Who are yours?
- Never have two faces in front of your team. Please don't say something in front of them and change your mind behind their backs. Keep consistent no matter what!
- Invest in leadership books and apply at least three strategies from that book.
- Commit today to become the leader you wish you had by understanding that leadership is all about people first and being a mentor for others.
- Commit today to stop condemning and criticizing people who face a challenging situation or are going through some

struggles. Make the time to listen to what they have to say and help them as much as possible. Also, try the Sandwich Method: Start with praise, then point out what needs to be improved, and close with another praise.
- Commit today to inspiring, motivating, and helping people get the job done. Make it clear that you work for them and not vice versa.
- Leadership is not about using your power to intimidate, scream, and make people feel less than themselves. Never, ever do that.
- Commit today to improve your communication and listening skills intentionally to become a better leader.

This last action will lead us to what it takes to become a great communicator. Follow me into the next chapter to learn the strategies and methods to develop your communication skills.

Check out the Appendix for the list of books that I highly recommend if you want to dig deeper into this subject.

Chapter 7

Develop Your Communication and Listening Skills

"There is a difference between listening and waiting for your turn to speak."
Simon Sinek

Communication

Your ability to communicate effectively can help you in any area of your life. In my career and personal life, I have encountered people who seem to get whatever they want more quickly than their peers. Those people were like magnets that attract the best opportunities, as they were the first who got a call when a client or prospect was looking for support; their colleagues, friends, and family members always want to be around them; and in a nutshell, it always seemed that all doors opened quickly for them.

I wanted to know why some people, despite their deep knowledge of a subject, never really get ahead or promoted. Still, on the other side, people with good knowledge or less are the ones who are readily accepted, valued, and promoted. I kept asking myself how that could be, and the following questions came into my mind over and over again:

- Is it because those people are more brilliant or competitive?
- Is it because of their good-looking physical appearance?
- Is it because of their education?

The good news is: The answer is *none of the above*. Through my research, I discovered everyone had one thing in common. They mastered communication.

I found out that getting ahead in life will always depend on how you communicate, listen, and get along with other people. One thing to note here is that to be a great communicator, you must be a great listener first. I know this is easier said than done. If you feel like you have to speak most of the time and get your ideas across, but are afraid to make mistakes or do not know how to do it effectively, you're not alone.

I cannot count the number of opportunities I have missed because of my lack of communication skills. I had poor communication skills and much poorer listening skills. I constantly interrupted people when talking in every event I attended. The same goes for home, where I didn't know how to communicate effectively with my children. When I asked them a question about their day at school, I immediately interrupted them as soon as they started talking, or I was thoroughly checked out by looking at my phone or distracted by other things. They finally got discouraged with me, and the next time I asked them about school, they answered with a vague, "Great, Dad!"

One time, I missed the opportunity to get a promotion because of my poor communication skills. The big trap I fell into was thinking that knowing my subject very well after a couple of years in that industry gave me the power to say whatever I wanted because I considered myself an expert without considering the feelings of my teammates. I didn't realize my poor communication was playing against me, and most importantly, my poor listening skills made people feel unheard, making them want to leave the project we were working on.

When I decided to change and improve my communication skills, to go from poor communication to excellent communication, I started asking myself the following questions:

- How do high achievers and successful people communicate?
- What books do they read on effective communication?
- What seminars do they attend to improve their communication?
- What about their body language when they communicate?
- What about their listening skills?
- Why do some people get promoted faster than others?

I didn't realize how communication could help someone climb the corporate ladder much faster than any other skill they may have, but all leaders I know communicate well and effectively. They understand that all our life issues and challenges can directly result from inappropriate and ineffective communication. All successful people and great leaders understand the power of words and the impact this can have in their relationships and professional careers; they know that the one who listens the most is the one who learns the most.

For example, my manager from the previous chapter never spoke about "the problem" we had. Instead, she used "challenge" or "opportunity" when we ran toward an issue. She always said: "What a great challenge! How can we fix it all together and learn from it?" She knew choosing a positive word versus a negative word would help us shift our minds to something more exciting, and we all then faced this challenge with a different approach.

Implementing Communication with my Daughters

Since I practiced a martial art named Nanbudo in secondary school, I encouraged my daughter to do the same when she turned six and enrolled in karate. Initially, she didn't look like she wanted to do it, which frustrated me immensely. Instead of communicating with her about why she didn't like it, I got frustrated and kept pushing her to do it. I ordered a book from Joe Ehrmann called *InSideOut Coaching* and read his book during her training session. This book made me realize I wasn't applying the correct strategies; I was more transactional in my coaching approach instead of being transformational. I realized that I expected her to do better than I did a decade back when I quit Nanbudo instead of understanding why she wasn't motivated to do it. Reading Ehrmann's book completely changed the way I was leading, coaching, and, most importantly, communicating with my daughters to become the best versions of themselves. Since that day, I decided to be transformational when communicating and coaching them.

In his book *Exactly What to Say*, Phil Jones shares twenty-three ideas and strategies that anyone can use to obtain the outcome they are looking for. This book is one of the first books I read, and I decided to apply the ideas he shared in the book. I started using it in my professional life, and I was hooked. After using these strategies, the results exceeded my expectations. People in my workplace started responding to me and were willing to help me most of the time. If I could get these results after reading one book on effective communication, what would happen if I read more books on that subject?

Listening

> *"One of the most sincere forms of respect is actually listening to what another has to say."*
> **Bryant H. McGill**

After reading one book and applying its tips, I knew I could achieve even more if I read other books on that subject. As you know, continuous learning and consistency are the keys to mastering anything! I decided to invest more time in that skill, as my next goal was to become a great listener. Every book I read on communication and listening skills had one thing in common: Great communicators are also deep listeners. Listening was not my strong suit. My knowledge increased when I began implementing the strategies and ideas I read in different books. As stated by Adam Grant in his book *Hidden Potential,* "The best leader is not the person who talks the most, but the one who listens best."

Listening profoundly and intentionally is the key to becoming a great communicator. In his book *How to Listen,* Oscar Trimboli provides valuable strategies anyone can apply to strengthen their listening skills. One strategy that really helped me was when he explained how to get ready to listen before a conversation or a meeting commences. For example, you can listen to yourself by focusing on your breathing (the slower you breathe, the stronger your listening will be) and removing all distractions around you (phone, radio, television, Outlook notifications).

I had never thought about getting ready to listen until I read his book, and maybe you're the same. The deal is simple: Anytime I have prepared myself to get ready before a conversation or a meeting starts, I feel more engaged and focused, and this, in turn, makes the person I am talking to feel understood.

Listening deeply beyond words and, at the same time, being physically and mentally present, helped me better understand what the other person was thinking even before they spoke or completed a sentence. Anytime I did it with total presence and focus, I could also see how they felt and their overall mood through their facial expressions.

I know it's not easy to become a good listener overnight; it takes time and practice. Learning how to listen effectively took me weeks, even months. I failed so many times by interrupting the person I was conversing with, but the good news is that I kept reminding myself that it is part of the process. I knew what I was trying to achieve in the long run, and I'm much closer to becoming a good, deep listener. I also understand this is an ongoing process; I have to stay focused and keep improving even though I have developed the habit of becoming a deep listener over time.

My suggestion for you is to first believe you can become a better listener and keep paying attention to what works best for you. When you try this for the first time, try to remove all distractions and stay calm when your colleagues, partner, friends, or children are speaking. Don't be distracted; stop doing what you have been doing and give him or her your undivided attention. Wait for one or three seconds when he or she is done before you answer. It also works well when you summarize what has been said or ask questions such as, "Is that what you meant?" or "My understanding about it is..." before answering.

Mastering your communication skills, which are associated with deep listening, will give you the secret weapon to reach the next level in your professional and personal life and, in turn, help you achieve more than your peers.

As you already know, it's not the one who talks the most who learns the most; it's the one who listens the most. So, become a world-class listener starting today and see how your life will change.

The more I read on that subject, the more I learned, the more I put it into practice, and the more fantastic results I got. Below is a short list of my lessons about effective communication and listening over the years.

Action Steps

- Great communicators are deep listeners. Commit today to become an active listener. You will be amazed at how much you will learn.
- Listen deeply with compassion and with your full attention. Resist the temptation to criticize, judge, condemn, or jump to conclusions.

- Practice the habit of not interrupting someone in the middle of a conversation.
- Keep eye contact while listening and show through your body language that you are fully engaged. Say something like, "Yes, I see," nod your head, etc. If not sure, rephrase and summarize what the other person was saying to show that you have understood.
- Practice not checking your phone or notifications while speaking with someone. Remove all distractions when talking with someone, and always give your full attention.
- Wait one to three seconds before you start talking when someone is done speaking.
- Remove negative words from your vocabulary and resolve today only to use positive and motivational words.

Once you know what needs to be done to go from point A to point B, you can make a plan, write down a goal to achieve in your list, and work on it daily. If I can do it, you can do it too. Communication skills are like any other skill—you can learn if you sincerely desire to improve.

Check out the Appendix for the list of books that I highly recommend if you want to dig deeper into this subject.

Chapter 8

Develop Your Selling Skills

The number-one skill I would recommend learning and getting good at is selling. Yes, you heard that correctly. Selling is a skill to learn for today and the future, regardless of your career path and ambitions. This could be:

- Negotiating a salary raise.
- Negotiating new contract agreements with potential customers or suppliers.
- Buying a new vehicle.
- Attracting a new business partner.
- Pitching new ideas to a potential partner.

Why? Because knowing how to sell gets you what you want. If you want a new job, you must know how to sell your knowledge and show an interviewer how it will help solve their problem. Some people sell themselves so poorly during the first interview they aren't considered for the second round.

Let's pretend you are a seller representative in an electronic store. If you want to sell a product to a customer, you will have to know how to sell that product and explain how the product is going to help solve their issue. If you want to try a new restaurant in town, but your spouse wants to see a movie, you will have to negotiate well and show your spouse the benefit of going to the new restaurant.

Developing your leadership and communication skills will give you a big advantage if you want to learn how to sell. In today's world, it doesn't matter where you live; face-to-face interaction is the preferred communication exchange between people despite the increased pace of technology. This is where selling comes into play. This is not a course on how to sell something but a quick guide and strategies that you can follow and get immediate results. If you are a professional seller, chances are you have already read a lot of books on selling. My goal is to awaken your awareness of this skill, which unfortunately is sometimes neglected by many of us, so that you can follow the same path I did. Selling is a learnable skill. If you learn the basics of selling you are about to discover, you will be better at selling and negotiating than 95 percent of the population.

This skill will help you show a potential prospect how your knowledge or product will help solve issues, increase your salary and hourly rate, and get more contracts with clients and possibly new prospects. It will also help you get more yeses in any other social activities.

Understand That Selling is Everywhere

Let's begin with these facts:

- As an employee, you have a job because a sale has already taken place. Top-selling people in your company worked very hard to win the project you're working on right now.
- If you are self-employed, you must sell your service to potential clients and show them how you can help solve their biggest issue.

- Even big companies like Apple and Microsoft are in the selling business, and the reason they are so successful is that they sell a lot of their products.

As Daniel Pink highlighted in his book *To Sell Is Human*, we are selling almost everything we do. To sell is to persuade someone of the value of your product or service.

As you already know, awareness is key. Before investing my time in this new skill, I started asking myself the following questions:

- Who are the experts in this field?
- What books do they read?
- What audio programs do they listen to?
- How many hours do I need to invest to become good at this skill?

Consistency is key. If you want to become good at anything, you're going to need to make a plan. Write it in your weekly schedule, then work on it regularly and consistently. Soon enough, I started to feel very comfortable with this skill.

Understand Your Most Valuable Asset is You

Let's say you're trying to buy a new laptop, and two different sales representatives approach you. You decide to pick one of them and buy the product. Do you remember why you chose that seller representative? What was the turning point that helped make your decision? For example, it could be because they asked good questions and listened carefully to your answers without interrupting you. This approach will help them identify your biggest problem and the perfect solution for this problem.

I remember when I was looking to buy a tablet. I didn't care about the brand. I just wanted to buy a decent tablet that would help me be more effective, especially during my business travel time. I first stopped by and looked over the Apple products. The seller representative who approached me didn't care about asking me what I was looking for, about the problem I wanted to solve, or why I was looking to buy a tablet.

"Hi, sir. This is a very good tablet. It's the one you're looking for. It's Apple, you know. Just buy it, and you won't regret it, I guarantee," the seller representative asked.

I greeted him back and just said that I was looking around. Then I moved on to the next stand.

The first lesson learned here is: Never forget that selling is about helping solve others' problems, and if done well, they will buy from you.

A couple of meters away, I stopped by the Microsoft products. The sales representative was the total opposite of his colleague. He greeted me with a huge smile on his face, asked me about my day, and asked how I had been doing so far. He then asked what I was looking for, showed me the different types of models, and took the time to explain each of them. Anytime he asked me a question, he listened carefully, and once I was done talking, he asked the next question, and the next question, and *another* one. Finally, he told me he had selected two models and wanted me to take my time to try them and see what fit the best. He then left me alone while I was trying each of them but did not stray too far, and he jumped right in when I had a question. He didn't bounce between customers, trying to sell his product to multiple people at once. Instead, he devoted his time to me. He made me feel like I was the most important customer.

In his book *The Irresistible Consultant's Guide to Winning Clients*, David A. Fields explains how thinking right side up will help you shift from thinking about your services, expertise, and problem-solving skills to thinking about your prospects' problems, needs, and situations. Thinking right side up is not about you but about the customer. It's not about your product, your skills, or your expertise but about your client's biggest problem, situation, aspirations, struggles, and wins. It's about understanding your customer's or prospect's needs and being able to ask a series of good questions that will help you first connect with them, and also find out what exactly is preventing them from sleeping at night, then craft the best possible solution that will help your customer or prospect to fix the problem and have a big win.

Between these two sales representatives working in the same electronic store, I could identify who was thinking right side up.

I realized that top sales representatives understand it's not about them, their product, their service, or their problem-solving skills when meeting a new prospect for the first time. It's all about the prospect—their needs, situations, and problems—and how the representative can help them the best. They do this by asking good questions and listening deeply. When I bought the Microsoft tablet, the difference was between the two sales representatives. I got a second confirmation that having the right approach by being friendly, asking good questions, listening carefully, and always having the customer's needs in mind will help you find the customer's problems and the solution to fix them.

After I read a book written by Jeb Blount, *People Buy You*, I was able to connect the dots with that day. In his book, Blount points out the five levers that cause people to buy from you, which are likability, connection, solving problems, building trust, and creating a positive emotional experience. Keep this key quote in mind: "The essence of business is one person solving another person's problem." This is fundamental to being a good seller. It all starts with *you*. Blount outlines it in great detail in his book. People will always buy *you* before buying from you.

Action Steps

- Resolve to invest several hours each week on learning the skill of selling.
- Read books written by experts (check the Appendix to see the books that helped me the most).
- Listen to audiobooks while driving to accelerate your learning curve.
- Commit today to apply these skills, which starts with always being likable by smiling, being respectful and friendly no matter what, asking good questions, listening carefully without interruption, and removing all distractions when talking to a prospect.
- Always think from the perspective of a prospect. Avoid making assumptions or jumping to conclusions. Instead, ask good questions, listen deeply, connect, build lasting relationships and trust, and pay attention to the little details that will, in turn, help you craft the best solution possible for your prospect.
- Resolve today to always go the extra mile. Always ask what you can do, how you can help, and how you can keep giving. Remember, the one who gives the most always wins.
- Resolve to treat every single person, prospect, and client as a one-billion-dollar customer. You never know who is watching.

Learning and applying these simple steps will help you develop your selling skills and advance your career and business. This is why I think selling is one of the most valuable skills and encourage you to invest in learning how to sell. Now that we have learned how to develop our leadership, communication, and selling skills, let's see how this can help us make more money and accelerate our path to financial freedom.

Check out the Appendix for the list of books that I highly recommend if you want to dig deeper into this subject.

Chapter 9

Attract, Make, Save, and Invest More Money

Disclaimer: In the following chapter as well as in this entire book, I'm just sharing my own experiences and how I overcame each of these challenges. Before taking any steps regarding how to make, save, and invest money, do your own research and seek professional advice.

It has never been this easy to make money. In the Golden Age of technology, we have many possibilities to make a lot of money. You can learn any skill if you want to, and you are just a click away on sites like Google, Udemy, Khan Academy, and YouTube. But sometimes there is no time to learn a new skill because of your family responsibilities and day job! You can still earn extra bucks that can help you make more money to save, invest, and pay your debt. In this chapter, you will see what I have done to go from having an urgent amount of debt, living paycheck to paycheck to pay off all my debt, to making more money and not worrying about my paycheck.

For as long as I can remember, I was always short on money despite being an engineer. Don't get me wrong, this is not to say engineers don't make good salaries. I'm just blaming myself for not knowing *how* to use my money *wisely* at the time.

If you are lucky enough to get hired by a good company after graduation, you can earn a good salary right at the beginning. Here I was with my degree in my pocket but zero knowledge of how to manage money. Where the hell should I have learned how to do such a thing? After spending six years in primary school, seven years in secondary school, and about five years in university, I spent about eighteen years in total of my life in the school system that didn't teach me how to manage money. The main concern I have is that nothing has changed since I left university.

The good news is you are about to learn what I have done to make, save, and invest money wisely. I will share with you the books I read and the strategies I have followed that have worked well for me. One thing I want to make clear is don't follow these people on social networks who make it sound like it is very easy to have a famous and glorious life. You must work very hard and consistently to get where you need to be.

Financial Literacy

> *"A person can be highly educated, professionally successful, and financially illiterate."*
> **Robert Kiyosaki**

As you already know, awareness is the key to success. Awareness will help you move from where you are to where you want to be if you are open to doing what is required to get there. For me, I knew that if I wanted to change my financial life, I needed to do something that I had never done before. So, I started reading every book on financial literacy that I could get my hands on and listened to audio podcasts on that subject.

One of the books that completely changed and improved my financial knowledge was the book *Rich Dad Poor Dad* by Robert Kiyosaki. This book taught me the strategies and principles the rich follow that the poor and the middle class do not. For successful people, it is all about acquiring assets, meaning everything that puts money back into your pocket, such as real estate investment (the money comes back with cash flow), stock market investment (the money comes back with a dividend payment), etc. On the other hand, middle-class and poor people are all about liabilities, meaning taking money out of their pockets, such as buying stuff like cars, big TVs, etc., that decrease in value over time.

Reading *Rich Dad Poor Dad* was a real eye-opener for me. I realized that I was spending my money on liabilities most of the time. I had urgent credit card expenses, lines of credit, car loans, etc. The amount of debt I had sometimes was so immense that I could barely make all the payments on time. Thankfully, this book, and many other books written by experts, awakened my awareness and put me on the path to successfully and intelligently making, saving, and investing my money.

In his book *The Total Money Makeover,* Dave Ramsey outlines practical steps (so-called baby steps) and techniques that anyone can use to set aside an emergency starter fund and explains how anyone serious about getting out of debt can apply to pay off all their debt, saving three to six months of expenses, investing about 15 percent for retirement, saving for children's tuitions, accelerating mortgage payments, and giving back to the community. I have applied the steps outlined in Ramsey's book to pay all my car loans, credit cards, and student loan debt, putting aside one year of my overall monthly expenses, saving and investing for my children's education, and investing for my retirement. Right now, I'm accelerating my mortgage payment. Were all the baby steps easy to follow? Not at all! It took me years to get to this point, but I knew deep inside me that this is the price to pay if you are serious about getting out of debt, saving, and investing. I had to delay as much as possible the gratifications and focus on my plan.

I finally had something to work with. As you know, what gets planned out can be measured and improved. Tony Robbins said respectfully: "Knowledge isn't power; it's potential power. Execution trumps knowledge any day of the week." I rapidly wrote down what needed to be done first, which was putting aside an emergency fund and paying off my debt. Writing my plan and goal down didn't stop there, and I knew I still had a good challenge to deal with now, but it was a good place to start. Sometimes, having too many insights and ideas is more confusing than helpful. But I knew one thing: I had to start and take action. After acquiring the knowledge I sought, I had to decide what to focus on first.

Knowing what I learned, it was time to take the first step and change the game, and logically, the first step for me was to set aside money for the rainy days before paying my debt. I didn't want to fall back to where I was (not saving money) just in case things didn't go as planned. I also knew having one to three months of payments set aside would give me peace of mind if something unexpected happened. While paying the minimum payment on my debt, my most significant focus was putting aside the equivalent of one month as quickly as possible. Once reached, I move to two and then three.

I knew deep inside that if something was going to change, I would have to take action, and I needed to take it now. So, I did. I wrote it down as a goal to pay myself first (about 10 percent of my bi-weekly paycheck), and added it to my monthly plan, then reviewed it regularly.

I revisited my plan every two weeks and made adjustments as necessary. During my monthly review, I looked at all my expenses and always tried to find a way to increase my savings. I looked at all the unnecessary stuff I bought that month and saw how they either helped me because it was necessary or were just the so-called "nice to have." I became aware of the tiny details month after month, which helped me increase my savings on the same occasion. The key here is to be mindful of how much money comes out of your pocket and for what intent. The best way to know how much money comes out of your pocket monthly is to download your credit card and bank statements. What also helped me was to stop using my credit card, except for big purchases. I took cash from my bank account every month and used it for the month. This approach can help you save as much money as possible, as you won't have your credit card to make any impulsive purchases.

I'm not asking you to stop using your credit card altogether, especially if you can pay off the balance at the end of each month or before the due date. But if you are like me and don't know how to control impulsive expenses, check if putting the credit card aside for a moment might be helpful. In my case, I had completely stopped using all my credit cards, including the one from Costco, during this period of my life. I did it because I knew that one day, it would pay off when I ultimately got out of my debt. Again, sometimes it's better to suffer a little bit by delaying gratification for a better future.

Seeing how the little sacrifices were starting to pay off, I went all in, and every time I received back my taxes, I used half of the amount to pay down my debts and saved the other half. In the past, I used this money to pay for more shiny toys. Every raise was divided in two, where half went to my debts and the rest to my savings accounts. I started side hustles to accelerate my debt payments, and I know that this, in turn, will dramatically increase my savings account. After twenty-two months, I paid off all nuisance debts such as line of credit, car loan, credit card. The total amount of these nuisance debts was around $38,000. Yes, you read it correctly, $38,000. Since then, I have accelerated my savings and investments. All of that was possible because I became aware of my situation. Was that easy? Hell no! But I knew that I needed to follow these steps to get my life back in control. If I can do it, you can do it too.

How to Attract Money

> *"If you want to have more, you have to become more. Success is not something you pursue. What you pursue will elude you; it can be like trying to chase butterflies. Success is something you attract by the person you become."*
> **Jim Rohn**

I listened to a podcast the other day from Jim Rohn during my workout in the gym. He said something that caught my attention: "Don't chase money. You attract money by the person you become." This made me think and reflect during my entire workout. I concluded that to attract more money into your life, you have to become more valuable in the market and take care of your health and personal well-being. In a nutshell, if you want to attract more money into your life, go back to the beginning of this book and apply and follow all the strategies and techniques I shared with you so far, and you will not only become a better *you*, but you will also attract a lot of money into your life. You can attract money by:

- Deciding today to make a list of the goals you want to accomplish and working toward your goals every single day.
- Improving your time management will help you maximize your productivity and impact.
- Working on your personal development by identifying the one skill that will help you the most and go all in by making a plan and investing in that skill every single day.
- Learning, studying, asking questions, seeking advice, becoming a sponge, and always learning from the expert. Once you master a skill, repeat the process and choose another one.
- Taking your physical fitness and personal well-being to the next level. You may ask yourself how this will help you attract

more money into your life. Let me tell you, improving your fitness will give you more energy to increase your focus and do more than your competition, but you will also experience a high level of overall health and well-being.
- By developing your leadership skills, you will help more people become leaders and help people you work with perform at a higher level than they imagined possible.
- By developing your communication and listening skills, you will not only improve the way you communicate with people, which in turn will give you more contracts if you are a consultant, but also help you get promoted more quickly if you are an employee. Your learning skills will dramatically increase, as the one who listens the most learns the most.

These are the strategies that I have followed to attract customers, clients, and references from people I have worked with in the past. I trusted the process, and I didn't think about the outcome. Step by step, things started to change for me. I think that if you are serious about taking back control of your life in terms of personal development, leadership, becoming a good communicator, and bringing your physical health to the next level, the strategies that I outlined in this book can help you get there, and, in turn, you will automatically attract money. Once you start to attract more money into your life, how do you even make more money if you want to? Let's dive in!

Make More Money

> "When your time spent making money is significantly greater than your time spent spending money, you will be amazed at how much you can save without even really thinking about it."
> **Sophia Amoruso**

I do not know about you, but anytime I read this quote, it takes me back to the start of my transformational journey. I was spending more money than I earned, and at the end of every month, it was very difficult for my family and me. This is not a good feeling, and I hope you will never experience it. I explained in the previous chapter how using your credit card without thinking can be detrimental to achieving your financial goal. I want to reiterate that even though this chapter covers how to make money, you must manage your expenses by cutting where possible. This will accelerate your savings and skyrocket your investments. We have endless opportunities to make money, and even though the list below is not exhaustive, this is what I have used in my own life.

a) Cutting Where You Can

It has never been as easy to make money as it is today. Look around you, check your bank statements, and get an idea of where your money flows most of the time. Back to the time when I didn't know how to make and manage my money, I just spent it all the time. All the books I have read on money and investment have the same primary principle when it comes to making more money: cutting your expenses. This step is crucial if you are serious about making and saving more money. It all starts with you. Get serious about this principle, as it will allow you to see how high your expenses are and where you can cut.

In general, check your expenses, and you will see how much you spend on food, clothes, restaurants, transportation, rent, etc. I'm not asking you to be frugal and stop living; I'm just saying that sometimes we complain that we wish we could make more money, but the solution is just in front of us. We can make a bit more money by cutting out the things we don't need regularly. Do we need to go to the restaurant every week or buy clothes and shoes every week? I will let you decide for yourself. All that I know is that cutting the stuff I didn't need helped me save more money. By cooking at home most of the time, we achieved two things: We saved more money and ate more healthy food. During the pandemic, we sold one of our cars, and by doing so, we saved more money on gasoline and maintenance.

b) Side Hustles and Side Businesses

As mentioned before, having a side hustle can help you make more money quickly. I firmly believe that no one should depend on one single job that provides only one single income these days. Everyone, no matter how much money they are making right now, still has the opportunity to make a bit more for themselves, which, in turn, will help them save and invest. You have multiple choices. You could start making some deliveries with Uber or DoorDash, start a side business like Amazon FBA, drop-shipping, or a YouTube channel, become a freelance writer or engineer, or launch a blog. The possibilities are endless to make a bit more money on the side. Let me repeat that again: Don't put all your eggs in the same basket in today's world. Find the time to work on your side hustle or side business while keeping your day job as long as you can, and do it until you can start living entirely from your side hustle or side business. Look at what happened during the pandemic; most people lost their jobs overnight and ended up with nothing. Don't let it happen to you.

c) Get the most out of your daily job and negotiate a raise at least once per year.

Another option to explore is making more money in your current full-time job. This can be done by maximizing your benefits, asking your boss to work remotely, or asking for a big raise. I missed all these points while working as an employee in my previous job. Because I wasn't more valuable for my company, guess what? I only ever got low raises that were, most of the time, below inflation. My former company made me travel a lot at one point in my career, but I still got the same paycheck. I didn't know that travel time and spending time away from my family could give me options to ask for more money. Because I wasn't confident enough to ask for more, I was making less. Why less? Taking into consideration the travel time of two to five hours (depending on if it was by car, train, or plane), plus hotel time, plus extended hours (more than ten to twelve hours for some days), my paycheck was the same, so my salary was lower. I was not coasting anymore and wasn't getting ahead at all. I was falling behind. But when I started working on myself, learning more, investing more, optimizing, and improving my time management, I gained more confidence and increased my salary more than I could imagine. Let's explore what our options are.

1. **Max out your company pension plan.** If your current company has a pension plan and it matches the percentage you're contributing, please do it. Most of the companies are willing to match up to 5 percent of the contribution of their employees. If that is the case, do it and take the full percentage contribution, as this is free money you're leaving on the table if you don't.
2. **Take full advantage of health and well-being benefits.** Check out what your employer is proposing and take full advantage of it. Sometimes, you have access to a good reduction in fitness, massage, orthopedic care, and speech

therapy for kids. The list goes on. Call your human resources representative and get all the information regarding your benefits. You might be surprised by the benefits you have and how they can help you in your daily life.

3. **Be aware of your hourly rate versus yearly salary.** Even if you are an employee, think like an entrepreneur. Always try to make more on an hourly rate. Don't only look at your yearly salary. Do the math, take into consideration your hourly rate, and see if it is really what you get paid after removing your commuting time, business-traveling time (if applicable), clothes, stress, and the time you need to get ready before you leave your house, etc. All of this time should be taken into consideration. You might be surprised by the results.

4. **Never miss the opportunity to ask for a second raise after the first official one in the same calendar year.** As the saying goes, no ask, no get. No risk, no reward. If you don't ask, the answer will automatically be a no. So, it is worth trying to ask. Get this: To hire you, human resources spends time and money to get you on board, and the company even spends more money to train you for the first months until you become fully independent. Do you really think that a company is willing to let you go after all the money they spend on you? I don't think so, and you shouldn't either. You are more valuable to your company than you may think. Do not be satisfied with only one yearly raise, especially if your raise is below inflation, which is what 95 percent of the employees get. To earn more, learn, and grow more, invest in yourself more than you do in your job. Learn that one skill that will make you more valuable for your company.

    a. Sit down with your boss and ask him to provide you with a list of what you should do to reach the next level and become a top performer for your organization.

b. Become very good at what you do and seek regular communication exchanges with your boss. Make sure that what you do and deliver is aligned with his or her expectations. Also, make sure that the colleagues you are working with daily appreciate your support and the way you communicate. Finally, make sure that everyone on the same level and those above you appreciate your work. How you do that is to overprepare for a meeting where you know that they will be present and overdeliver. The goal here is to ensure that when your boss or human resources goes back and checks how you behave, how well you work with others, and/or how productive you are, all of them will have a positive appreciation of all those characteristics.

c. Send a weekly summary of your achievements every Friday where you will specify the following:
- Highlight your achievements from the prior week. Make sure to explain what you did very well.
- List your challenges and how you plan to overcome them. Feel free to request support and help if needed.
- Regarding the upcoming activity and deliverables you plan to do for the week ahead, ask your boss to add any other activity he/she would like you to take care of.

d. Have a one-on-one project review once per month and make sure that what you are working on is still your boss's top priority. In this fast-paced world, things change very fast, and yesterday's priority might not be today's priority anymore. So, be careful and keep that in mind.

e. Check your market value on Glassdoor and LinkedIn, and don't be afraid to contact the headhunter company and ask for your market value. Once you have all this data, use it during the conversation with your boss. Check Item 3 above to be more accurate when asking for your raise.

f. After a couple of years in the same company, people, including your boss, take you for granted. Getting another job offer will be a game-changer for you.

Note: If you are valuable to your boss and company, they will do everything under their control to get you a good raise. They know, as do the company's human resources, that replacing you will cost them more money.

5. **Work remotely**. I seriously think that if someone controls your time, they also indirectly control what and when you can earn a bit extra money. If you have to be in the office more than two days a week, it might be difficult for you to earn extra money during this time. If your job permits, ensure you work 100 percent remotely if you want total control of your time. This will save you a lot of time commuting, getting ready for the job, buying clothes, and dealing with the stress that comes with it. If you have to go to the office, your boss has control of your time, which isn't good for increasing your income. To be financially independent in a relatively short time, you need to earn more in a relatively short period. To do this, you need to have the possibility of earning more money next to your nine-to-five. And this is only possible if you have total control of your time.

Save and Invest More Money

"It's not how much money you make, but how much money you keep, how hard it works for you, and how many generations you keep it for."
Robert Kiyosaki

Now that you know how to make more money, the question is how to save and invest wisely and take intelligent and calculated risks with that money.

Warren Buffett states two rules of investment: one, don't lose money, and two, don't forget rule number one. If there is one thing I didn't know, it was Buffett's rules. I still remember the first time I opened a TFSA (Tax-Free Saving Account) and an RRSP (Register Retirement Saving Plan) at my bank. The financial advisor asked me a set of questions and, based on that, identified my risk tolerance and shared it with me. It took approximately one hour each to complete this exercise for TFSA and RRSP. The papers showed that my risk tolerance was conservative and that my hard-earned money would be invested in mutual funds. I was filled with pride when I left the bank that day. What I didn't know was the fees I would pay every year, no matter how my portfolio would perform. Whether it performed poorly or well, the 4 to 5 percent of fees would still be deducted from my account. Furthermore, I had no idea what I was investing in. I knew nothing about stocks versus bonds and why the financial advisor chose that stock over others that day. I was completely checked out, and I wished the financial advisor could have helped me a bit more. Looking back on that experience, he was doing his job, meaning doing what he was getting paid for. I learned during my transformational years to never blame anyone for my poor choices. It was on me to be prepared and learn how to invest instead of giving my hard-earned money to someone I didn't know. I decided to read all the books on that subject so it would never happen to me again. You can do the same thing.

Remember, this is your money; if you don't care for it, no one will do it for you. Please don't tell me the financial advisor from your bank has your best interest in mind. They are just doing their job and have a dozen clients they have to take care of every day. They completely forgot about you when you stepped out of their office. Take full responsibility and take back the total control of your money.

To go from average to the next level in terms of understanding how to save and invest my money intelligently, I followed the same principles:

- What books on investing do the experts read?
- What podcasts do they listen to?
- How much time should I invest to go to the next level?
- Which online courses should I invest in?

Once I asked myself these questions, I went all in. I identified the books I should read and the hours I should invest every week and wrote them down in my planner. The books I read all covered three main principles: your number, fees, and portfolio asset allocation.

- **Your number**

    What is your ideal retirement number? In his book *The Automatic Millionaire*, David Bach said this: "If you don't know where you're going, you might not like where you end up." Knowing your number will give you the awareness to work toward your goal daily and weekly. In my opinion, it's crucial to know the number you want to reach to achieve your retirement, as this will help you know the amount of money you need to have in your investment so that you can live off it during your retirement. My ideal and safe retirement number is about one million two hundred thousand dollars. It is not an exact science, as life happens, and things can change rapidly. The goal is to reach a number where you will no longer have to work. How do you come up with your number? Simple. Let's say you decide to retire at age sixty-five. Look at your current monthly expenses (this number will likely be less, as I take into consideration that all your big purchases will be already paid, like house, car, etc.), multiply your current monthly expenses (if we want to be conservative) by twenty or twenty-five, and you will get your ideal retirement number.

- **Your fees**

    Do you know how many fees your current investment portfolio costs you every year? Are you investing in an actively managed mutual or low-cost index fund? For many years, I paid many fees until I realized that it should not be that way. Make the time to check where you are investing and try to eliminate or reduce your fees as much as possible. In his masterpiece book *MONEY Master the Game*, Tony Robbins explains the impact your fees can have on your overall investment portfolio. Tony explained in great detail how big the difference is between someone paying 1 percent fees versus someone paying 3 percent. The higher your fees, the longer you may work to meet your magic retirement number. Please make the time to check this out and readjust. Again, don't trust your financial advisor when they look you in the eyes and say it is just 3.5 percent fees. These 3.5 percent fees add up over twenty years and will cost you a lot of money.

- **Portfolio asset allocation**

    Do you know how much of your money has been invested in stocks? How much in bonds? If you say yes, then good for you. I didn't know where or how my money was invested, which might be the case for many people. Based on your risk tolerance, the allocation of stocks versus bonds should be done carefully. Please take the time to read and learn about this topic before making your choices. Don't just be a follower; be a student. Take the information, read it, and select only what you understand. It has never been as easy to learn about this topic as it is today. You are one click away from getting a lot of information on the subject from YouTube. Diversification is key if you are looking for a long-term investment.

Once you have decided how your asset allocation plan will look—for example, 70 percent stocks and 30 percent bonds—rebalance it at least once a year to keep the same asset allocation. The market fluctuates throughout the year, and your original asset allocation might become 80 percent stocks and 20 percent bonds based on this fluctuation. I'll say it again: Look at your portfolio at least once a year and rebalance it if necessary.

What did I learn from the experts?

- I learned that successful people always think like entrepreneurs (most of them are), and even though they work for someone else, they refuse to see themselves as an employee. They understand that being an entrepreneur comes with many advantages, like tax reduction, being your boss, doing only stuff you love, not being stuck with a nine-to-five job, etc.
- I learned that successful people make the time to read, learn how to invest in the stock market, and don't trust a financial advisor guru to manage and grow their hard-earned money.
- I learned that successful people know that paying high fees will cost them more money in the long run, so they invest in a portfolio with a meager fee.

- I learned that successful people have multiple sources of income. They know that reaching their financial freedom as quickly as possible is only possible if they have multiple sources of revenue.
- I learned that successful people buy and invest in a combination of assets (stock markets, real estate, private equities, etc.). They follow Ray Dalio's advice and apply the holy grail of investing, a portfolio of eight to twelve uncorrelated (or non-correlated) investments that dramatically reduce risk without sacrificing returns.
- I learned that successful people are lifelong learners and see everyone as a teacher. They spend a lot of time reading, trying, failing, getting back up, and persevering.
- I learned that successful people not only automate their savings but also increase the amount of money they save every three months. They understand the power of compounding interest and how a quick increase of just 1 percent of their savings every three months is a game-changer.
- I learned that successful people stay in the stock market when everyone else leaves. They know you only lose money when you sell (especially if the market is down). Instead of getting out, they even buy more stock at a discount.
- I learned that successful people don't buy what the gurus sell everywhere, meaning they save 10 percent (up to 20 percent if they can) monthly and coast. They increase their income to increase their savings percentage to 25, 30, 40, 50 percent, and more. They know that staying with 10 percent savings won't give them financial freedom quickly.
- I learned that successful people understand that our time is finite, but the money accumulation is infinite. They use their time wisely and protect it at all costs, as they know that once time is gone, it's gone forever. No amount of money can repurchase your time.

Action Steps

- Commit today to start a side hustle to increase your income.
- Max out your TFSA account.
- Max out your RRSP and get tax benefits at the end of the year.
- Max out your employment retirement account, especially if your employer matches your contribution. It's free money.
- Find a way to make more money by:
- Cutting out what you don't use anymore in your house.
- Asking for a raise. Find a way to have a side hustle next to your nine-to-five job.
- Read every book about making, saving, and investing more money. (See the Appendix to get some book recommendations.)
- Check your portfolio fees and resolve today to eliminate or reduce your fees as much as possible.
- Read and learn about asset allocation before choosing stocks, bonds, etc. Make sure to allocate funds across different asset classes, like stocks and bonds. Follow Dalio's advice with the holy grail of investment.
- Make sure your financial advisor works in your best interests and not against you.

With all the strategies we have developed so far, knowing how to develop the habits that will help you maximize each one is crucial to reaching the next level. Follow me into the next chapter.

Check out the Appendix for the list of books that I highly recommend if you want to dig deeper into this subject.

Chapter 10

Habits and Routines

"Ninety-five percent of everything you do is the result of habits."
Aristotle

Are your current habits moving you closer to your goals or pulling you away? Good habits—like waking up early, eating clean, staying active, learning daily, saving money, and prioritizing family—require consistent effort and delayed gratification. On the other hand, habits like oversleeping, eating junk food, excessive TV, neglecting savings, or drinking heavily can hinder your progress. Take a moment to evaluate: Are your habits aligned with achieving your most important goal?

Good habits are the foundation for success; bad habits are why we stay stuck in life.

Before starting this journey to become the best version of myself, I was living my life on autopilot. I woke up late, got ready for work, started my day with easy tasks, and consciously avoided the most difficult ones. I drank coffee with colleagues and took short breaks regularly throughout the day. I often brought work home and worked for a couple of hours at night. Then I watched television and went to bed very late, leading me to wake up very late, and I just started over again.

And, oh, what did I do during the weekend? I went out Friday night, returned early Saturday, and slept almost until noon. Nothing was accomplished on Sunday either. I didn't really have a plan. I just went through the weekend like a zombie. I have to confess that writing this right now is very hard for me, as it is difficult to see how disconnected I was, but I know that sometimes you have to get through the most challenging times before changing the entire course of your life. Fortunately, I took back control of my life, and if I can do it, guess what? So can you.

Weekends are for relaxation, but the best ones come from planning. Treat your weekend like your workweek by writing down three to five activities for Saturday and Sunday. This ensures your time aligns with your values—rest, recovery, family, or fun—and helps you feel refreshed and ready for the week ahead. Don't leave your weekend to chance; plan it for maximum rejuvenation.

As you already know, self-awareness is critical to achieving great things in life. Like all other strategies and tactics I have shared throughout this book, I started asking myself the following questions:

- What habits have successful people implemented and follow every single day?
- What books do they read?
- What podcasts do they listen to?
- What can I do right now to get there?
- What do I need to stop doing daily that is not aligned with my goals?
- What one thing can I start doing today that will put me on the path of success?

I realized successful people all have a few common denominators: a commitment to daily habits that foster personal development, productivity, physical workout, well-being, and fulfillment. Here are a couple of them:

- Successful people have a great evening routine that sets up the end of the day and prepares them for a great night's sleep. They know that having a great night's sleep will allow them to start the following day earlier.
- They have a morning routine that they follow every single week.
- They have habits that help them go through their most important tasks and activities of the day.
- They focus on implementing good habits daily and replacing bad ones, as they know that good habits will open the door to greatness, while bad ones will make them miserable a couple of years from now.
- They have a weekend routine where they plan exactly what to do, starting Friday afternoon through Saturday and Sunday. By doing this, they know that these tiny weekend habits will help them rest, recover, and relax to be more present and focused the following week.

I heard a quote the other day while driving to the grocery market. Brian Tracy quoted Mark Matteson: "Good habits are hard to form and easy to live with. Bad habits are easy to form and hard to live with." This is exactly what happened to me a couple of years ago; all I had developed was bad habits. I didn't realize that:

- The habit of not saving money consistently was easy to form because I didn't want to delay instant gratification, but later on, it would be very difficult for me to have a good life because I wouldn't have enough money.
- Eating a lot of junk food tasted good at the moment and satisfied my instant gratification of having, for example, French fries, but I missed the fact that all this junk food would compound over time.

- Not developing the habits to learn and study every single day was easy to live with at that moment but very hard in the long run, as I would not only fall behind but also get stuck with a lower salary since my contribution and impact were so little.

Bad habits can be replaced with good ones through effort, discipline, and consistency. As Robin Sharma explains in *The 5AM Club*, research from University College London shows it takes at least sixty-six days to install a new habit. For example, it took me about seventy days to make waking up at 5:00 a.m. automatic—now, I wake up around 4:45 a.m. for extra personal time. Building a nightly routine took me fifty-five days, and drinking eight to ten glasses of water daily became a habit in just thirty days. It wasn't easy at first, but with persistence and strategies like keeping my alarm in another room, I made these changes stick.

> *"You'll never change your life until you change something you do daily. The secret of your success is found in your daily routine."*
> **John C. Maxwell**

All this is to say that the bare minimum is sixty-six days to create good habits that can change your life. But as you can see, it took me thirty to seventy days to implement a new habit. Try this and stick with it until you reach the point of automaticity. Depending on the habit you're trying to install, it may take you less than three weeks or more than six weeks. Repetition and repetition are key to implementing a new habit. The first few days will be tough; this is where most people, the average people, stop, but you are not average. Keep pushing, remind yourself of your *why*, and keep going until you reach the point of automaticity. Remember, if I can do it, you can do it too. Keep pushing.

Following all the strategies I'm sharing here with you helped me implement new habits and, more importantly, install morning, daily, weekly, and nightly routines. It wasn't easy, but I knew I had to do it to give myself a chance to succeed and regain control of my life.

Morning Routine

"Morning is an important time of day, because how you spend your morning can often tell you what kind of day you are going to have."
Lemony Snicket

It is crucial how you spend the first few hours of your morning. Most successful people start their day earlier because they know that a great morning routine can set the tone for the rest of the day. Implementing a great morning routine as a new habit would be best for becoming more productive and getting more things done than the average person.

Below, I would like to share a simple and proven strategy that you can use right now to implement a great morning routine:

- Plan your day the night before. Make a list of things you need to get done for the day and prioritize them.
- Go to bed earlier and aim for seven to eight hours of sleep.
- Wake up at or around 5:00 a.m.—the earlier, the better—and give yourself at least two hours to work on yourself before you officially start your workday. My morning routine looked like this:
    - 4:45 a.m.: wake-up time, get ready for my workout, drink a glass of water and meditate for ten minutes.
    - 5:00 to 6:00 a.m.: intense workout while listening to audiobooks.
    - 6:00 to 7:00 a.m.: read, learn, absorb good materials, and write.

- 7:00 to 8:00 a.m.: help my daughters get ready for school.
- 8:00 a.m.: start my workday.

Daily Routine

"The secret of your future is hidden in your daily routine."
Mike Murdock

- Always start your day with your most important task.
    - *Eat That Frog*, as Brian Tracy calls it in this book title.
    - 90/90/1 rule, as coined by Robin Sharma.
- Block undisturbed time in your calendar and get focused.
- Eliminate all sources of distraction, such as your cell phone and Outlook notifications. Clean your desktop. Remove all open sites that are not required for the work you plan to do.
- Plan and block three times daily to look at your emails. Here is what I do:
    - First round of email checks from 11:00 to 11:30 a.m. Here, make sure to prioritize very quickly what emails are urgent and essential from what can be delegated and eliminated.
    - The second round of email checks is from 3:00 to 3:30 p.m.
    - Third round of email checks is from 5:00 to 5:30 p.m. This last round allows me to see what can be added to my plan for the next day and what I can delegate or eliminate.
- Starting at 5:30 p.m., I reserve time for my well-being and my family.

If you want this great morning routine habit, follow these steps and stick with it for the next four weeks. There is no fast track to it; you have to work on it step by step every day. Start to wake up ten minutes earlier than usual and work your way up.

Nightly Routine

> *"If we want to live a wholehearted life, we have to become intentional about cultivating sleep and play, and about letting go of exhaustion as a status symbol."*
> **Brené Brown**

To function optimally all day long, we must have a great night's sleep, and the goal here is to aim for seven to eight hours. Let's face it: If you want to wake up earlier and start your day strong, you need to sleep well to allow your body to rest and recover. Below are the simple strategies that help me sleep well, and I hope they will also help you. Let's dive in:

- End your day with a recovery activity such as walking, getting a massage, or doing yoga.
- Drink tea to wind down, preferably no-caffeine tea like rooibos or chamomile.
- Have your last meal at least three hours before bed.
- Drink water one to two hours before bed.
- No TV, no surfing on the internet, no white screen one to two hours before bed.
- No alcohol at all from Monday to Friday.
- Relax your body before bed at least twice a week.
- Take the time to meditate, even if it's only for ten to twenty minutes before bed.
- Cool your room before bed. Check and see what temperature works best for you. For me, eighteen to nineteen degrees Celcius is ideal.

- Remove all digital devices in your room before bed.

Weekend Routine

"Weekends are time to recharge your batteries and refocus on the things that matter most."
Tony Robbins

For years, I wasted weekends on late nights, drinking, and low-quality activities, leaving me unprepared for the week ahead. Awareness became the turning point, helping me replace bad habits with intentional planning. By carefully organizing my weekends, I shifted from aimless time to purposeful plans for family, friends, and personal growth. Observing how successful people maximize their weekends inspired me—they approach weekends differently, using them to recharge and realign with their goals:

- Know that to be more productive during the week, you need to get as much rest as possible. Resting plays a vital role in their weekend routine.
- They sleep longer, listen to their body, and get as much rest as possible throughout the weekend.
- They spend the weekend with their family, cooking together, taking a long walk, watching a film, etc.
- They also block some undisturbed time during the weekend to do work around the house with their children. The children like it, but they also learn how to become good at fixing stuff manually.
- They block an undisturbed time to catch up with their closest friends and socialize about their journey, struggles, wins, and goals. As they know, the leader who shares and asks questions the most is the leader who wins.

- On Sunday, they plan the following week for the first hours of the day, as they know more than everyone else that a week is won the Sunday before. By planning the upcoming week on Sunday, they set themselves up for success.

Having this awareness helps me set up my week wisely. With persistence and consistency, I finally found a plan that worked for me and my family. Here is what my weekend plan looks like:

- Most of the time, I sleep until 8:00 a.m.
- Read for one hour Saturday and Sunday morning. I read books on entrepreneurship, leadership, investment, personal development, health and well-being, etc.
- Write for one hour Sunday morning. I like this activity, as it helps me improve my writing. I write on different subjects, such as personal development and time management.
- Family time takes up the rest of the day on Saturday and Sunday. For example, Saturday from 11:00 a.m. to 2:00 p.m., I drive my daughters to swimming activities, and at night is movie time. Generally, on Sunday afternoon, we spend some time together playing board games.
- I spent one hour planning the upcoming week, usually Sunday morning, which now takes me less than one hour.
- Socialization time with friends is one to two hours, mainly on Saturday afternoons. During this time, I catch up with a friend either by phone or spend some time together at his or my house. Housework is done mostly on Saturday morning for one to two hours. This could be cleaning the house or cutting the lawn.
- On weekends, I dedicate three hours to rest, reflect, and recover. This usually includes a one-hour walk in the woods with an audiobook or a run. Sometimes, I enjoy a coffee

at Starbucks while reflecting on the past week, planning improvements for the next, and journaling any new ideas. Resting happens throughout the day, simply lying down and letting my mind wander.

See what suits you best and plan your weekend effectively. There is no "right" weekend routine. It all depends on your priorities and how you want to spend your weekend. The goal here is to take intentional breaks from your work by engaging in activities that bring you joy, energy, and fulfillment. I hope what I have shared about how my weekend looks will inspire you to craft your own plan for the best possible weekend and help you identify what you value the most in terms of social activity and family activity. Remember that it will take some time until you find what suits you best. The first time won't be easy at all because you are trying to install a new habit by removing an old one. But keep pushing; if it were easy, everyone would do it. Take the time you need to implement this new habit, but also note that consistency is key, and it only works when you also develop self-discipline that will help you reach the next level. Let's find out what it takes to develop strong self-discipline.

Power of Self-Discipline

> *"The ability to make yourself do what you should do when you should do it, whether you feel like it or not."*
> **Elbert Hubbard**

Steady optimized routines and habits are key to getting ahead in life, but this will only work if you have the self-discipline to stay in the game longer than anyone else. Self-discipline is the secret weapon all successful people have. It's what separates top performers from average performers. Without self-discipline, the chance of you reaching the next level is close to zero. What separates high achievers from the rest is that they do it even though they don't feel like it.

Implementing self-discipline was very hard at the start. Even with a tremendous weekly plan and routine, I struggled to stay on course because of my lack of self-discipline. It was only when I forced myself to do what I had planned that things started to change. I realized self-discipline is about beginning a task and continuing it until it is completely done before moving to the next one. In the beginning, I was trying to do multiple tasks simultaneously, and if you try to catch up on two things simultaneously, you will catch up on none of them.

For example, if you start working on your most important task for the day, remove all distractions and go all in until the task is completed. Don't try to check your emails while working on something else. I learned the hard way, as my reports were filled with errors. I was so focused on doing and repeating the same things over and over that I didn't realize the amount of time it was taking me to return to my main task. Acting like that made it almost impossible for me to be in a flow state.

In a nutshell, multitasking does not work. Multitasking is a myth that exists only in movies. To regain control of your life and become its architect, stop multitasking and focus on one task at a time.

I often see people juggling tasks—checking emails, replying to messages, and chatting with colleagues—all at once. This only leads to errors, unfinished work, and wasted time. True success lies in focusing on one task at a time. Block time for specific activities, like reading emails or tackling your priorities, and give them your full attention. Stay disciplined and consistent, even when no one is watching, because you're working toward something bigger than yourself.

Alan Stein Jr. explains the principle of unseen hours in his master book, *Raise Your Game*. These are the unseen hours you spend working on your craft that no one seems to see. This is the time no camera, friend, or manager will ever be aware of. During these early morning struggles when the world is asleep, you can work intensely on yourself and your craft.

This makes me think about a soccer game. We see a beautiful stadium, clean, clinically cutting lawns, all lights are working perfectly, and all looks great. But you don't see all the technicians, engineers, and workers who clean the place, ensure that the lights are functioning well, cut the lawns, and so on. These are the unseen hours when no one was there to praise and applaud them.

My unseen hours begin at 4:45 a.m. with a morning routine focused on self-improvement. I start with a glass of water, ten minutes of meditation, and a 60 minutes workout that includes rope jumps, push-ups, kettlebell swings, HIIT, and stretching—hydrating and listening to a podcast or audiobook as I go. Afterward, I plan my day and spend thirty minutes studying my field, followed by thirty minutes writing. By 7:00 a.m., I get my daughters ready for school, and by 8:00 a.m., I'm ready to start my workday.

During my morning routine, I focus on the tiny progress I'm making, and not on the outcome. Waking up consistently helped me to only focus day in and day out on the process and stick with it. The name of the game here is to develop the self-discipline to be consistent with your routine for an extended period, and the outcome will take care of itself. I don't try to control the outcomes or the things that are far outside my control. Rather I stay consistent with the process. I learned from Jon Gordon that there are only four things that you have total control of every day: effort, attitude, behavior, and action.

By developing awareness and self-discipline, you will stop worrying about things outside your control zone. You will stop wasting your time and energy on what other people think about you, if you will still have a job two weeks from now, or if the weather will be great during your vacation time. Instead, focus your energy on the process. Develop self-discipline to keep working consistently on your personal development, communication and listening skills, saving money, and learning new skills. Keep doing it daily, and you will naturally set yourself up for success.

Action Steps

- Commit today to install a morning routine and the self-discipline to stick with it for a long period until you reach the point of automaticity.
- Commit today to install a daily routine and the self-discipline to stick with it for a long period until you reach the point of automaticity.
- Commit today to install a nightly routine and the self-discipline to stick with it for a long period until you reach the point of automaticity.
- Commit today to install a weekend routine and the self-discipline to stick with it for a long period until you reach the point of automaticity.
- Commit today to develop all the good habits and self-discipline that will help you work toward your goals in terms of personal development, learning a new skill, physical fitness, well-being, and mastering your listening and communication skills.

Consistency and discipline are key to reaching your goals faster. Habits like sleeping seven to eight hours, eating healthy, exercising, resting, and napping build long-term strength. What sets winners apart isn't action when it's easy—it's showing up when it's hard. Heroes are made by choosing to walk in the rain or snow, or adapting with a gym workout or push-ups when plans change. High achievers refuse to skip their commitments or make excuses. Self-discipline, like saving consistently to hit financial goals, separates those who achieve freedom from those who don't.

All we have developed so far will not work if you consistently make poor decisions. Making good choices consistently is what it takes to become the person you were meant to be. How do you make good choices? Let's figure this out in the following chapter.

Check out the Appendix for the list of books that I highly recommend if you want to dig deeper into this subject.

Chapter 11

The Power of Your Choices

Let's start this chapter with the following questions:

- How often have you made courageous goals on the last day of the year and dropped the ball by February 1st?
- How often have you chosen to stay in a job you hated because you haven't put enough money on the side to leave?
- How often have you chosen to stay in an unhealthy relationship?
- How often have you chosen to stay on a team where no one appreciates, values, or motivates you?
- How many times have you chosen not to become more valuable in the market?
- How often have you chosen not to save more money for your future because you didn't want to delay gratification?
- How often have you chosen to watch another episode from your preferred series on Netflix instead of reading something educational?
- How often have you chosen to look at your notifications while conversing with your spouse, partner, children, teammate, or coworker?

I suggest you reread the above and let it sink in a bit. This list is not exhaustive, and you can add additional questions that may have prevented you from making good choices and impacted your life negatively. Please take thirty minutes to reflect on these questions and see how these tiny choices you make unconsciously can significantly impact your life. Then do these steps:

- Write Down Your Questions: Take a piece of paper and write down all the questions that have prevented you from making good choices. Be honest with yourself—no one is judging you.
- Be Honest: It may be challenging at first, but trust yourself. Write down everything that comes to mind without holding back.
- Reflect and Answer: Go to each question and give your honest answer. For example, if you're wondering why you doubt yourself, explore the root cause of that fear.
- Commit to Change: Remember, we're letting go of the old you. Today is the day you take control and start making better choices moving forward.

Below is an example of what this process looks like:

- Question: "How often have I chosen to stay in a job I hate?"
- Possible Answer: "So often, because I didn't have enough money in my bank account and I'm not confident enough to find a new job."

I suggest you do this for all of the questions you wrote down. Just doing this one simple exercise can change your life for the better and put you on the path to becoming the architect of your life.

Every day, every week, every month, and every year, we have plenty of choices to make. Each decision we make will either guide us toward our goals or move us away from them.

Before I started working on myself and taking control of my life, I was making a lot of these choices. I wouldn't say all of these choices were bad, but I can say that most of them were terrible.

- I chose to eat junk food.
- I chose not to save more money.
- I chose not to write and work toward achieving my goals.
- I chose not to invest in my personal development.

Now that we understand how to identify why we made bad choices and work toward making better choices, let's now move on and see how making a sum of good decisions can help us move ahead and ultimately transform our lives.

The Sum of Our Choices

> *"Your life is the sum result of all your choices, both consciously and unconsciously. If you can control the process of choosing, you can take control of all aspects of your life. You can find the freedom that comes from being in charge of yourself."*
> **Robert F. Bennett**

When I was younger, I didn't realize our lives were the accumulation of our choices. But that's the truth. Where we are today is the sum of all the choices we made in the past. If we do not like where we are today, we must make better choices. And to make better choices, we must first be aware of our situation. We need to have a close, hard look at ourselves to determine where we want to go and how to get there. This self-awareness will help us make better decisions in the future.

The moment I understood clearly that the sum of our choices will shape our lives, destinies, and futures, everything shifted inside me. I understood that I constantly made bad choices; I was jeopardizing my future.

You are the architect of your life. Starting today, you need to accept full responsibility for your choices, and where you are right now in your life. Instead of complaining about the bad choices you made in the past, having regrets, beating yourself up as to why you did not take that opportunity when it showed up, and stressing about how little you have in your bank account, start working relentlessly to change everything in your life you don't like. Take full responsibility and work on yourself every single day. Fall in love with the process, and develop the self-awareness that will help you make better choices in the future.

Are you making the right choices?

> *"Better awareness leads to better choices, and better choices lead to better results."*
> **Robin Sharma**

Are you making the right choices? Are they aligned with your objectives and goals? If we are serious with ourselves, we can say the person we are today is the sum of all the choices we have made in the past. Please remember that every choice you make will have an urgent impact on your life, this can be translated to a bright future or a very difficult one. You're one choice away from becoming successful and changing your life, impact, and income. Here are some choices you encounter each day:

- You have the choice to read for one hour every day or spend that time on Netflix.
- You have the choice to work without distractions or to be surrounded by them.
- You have the choice to start saving money or to spend it on shiny, new toys.
- You have the choice to get yourself a gym membership or to eat junk food.

- You have the choice to learn a new skill that will help you dominate your domain, or to find excuses and do nothing.
- You have the choice to actively listen to your family and coworkers or to play with your device.
- You have the choice to wake up every morning a bit earlier and go through your morning routine or to spend more time in bed.
- You have the choice to take absolute responsibility for your actions or to complain, blame, and find more excuses.
- You have the choice to plan your day the night before or let the day plan you.
- You have the choice to work on your most important task first thing in the morning or to do things that are easy and fun.
- You have the choice to work every single day on a better future or to stay a prisoner of your past.

As we can see, developing self-awareness is essential to go from average to high achiever. Try to become very good at it; soon enough, you will see a massive change in your life in terms of personal development, fitness, and savings. It's not easy to make good choices on the spot; it takes time—and that's okay! The main objective here is to become aware of every decision you must make daily and select the right one. With all you have learned in this chapter, it's time to make that choice.

Action Steps

- Resolve to take a hard look at your life today and develop the self-awareness that will help you make the right choices moving forward.
- Commit to making the choices that are aligned with your saving goals and financial freedom.

- Commit today to making choices that are aligned with your personal development goals.
- Commit today to making the choices that are aligned with your physical health and personal well-being goals.
- Commit to choosing to learn a new skill every year.
- Commit to making better choices in terms of your leadership and impact.
- Track your progress and make necessary adjustments to stay on track as you move forward with it. Don't let success be a chance.

To make good choices consistently, you must be intentional about developing the self-awareness to guide you. This starts with accepting 100 percent responsibility for where you are and what you've done. It's up to you to change what you don't like in your life. Every choice, good or bad, is yours to own. You have everything within you to change the course of your life and become who you were meant to be. But this is only possible if you take control and resolve today that your choices are your responsibility—no matter the circumstances or what others say.

Resolve to only make the choices aligned with your goals, your personal development, your health, your savings, your impact, and so on. Remember, the choices you make today will shape your future positively or negatively. *Your choice!*

Check out the Appendix for the list of books that I highly recommend if you want to dig deeper into this subject.

Chapter 12

Eliminate Fear and Procrastination

"I've missed more than 9,000 shots in my career. I've lost almost 300 games. Twenty-six times, I've been trusted to take the game-winning shot and missed. I've failed over and over and over again in my life. And that is why I succeeded."
Michael Jordan

Almost every day, I talk with people who are afraid of something. Fear can stem from concerns like losing a job, missing a promotion, or not getting vacation time. It may also arise from staying in a stressful, unappreciated job, or from uncertainty about returning to school for a certification while juggling family responsibilities. There's fear of change, like moving to a new job or accepting a new opportunity, and worry about not being prepared for or failing an exam.

Because of these fears, people keep waiting for a better moment to speak up and take action. But guess what? This better moment will never come.

Do the above fears speak to you? If so, you are not alone. Fear needs to be taken seriously, as the lack of action related to fear can completely paralyze your life and prevent you from reaching the next level in terms of personal development. In a nutshell, the fear of failure might be the reason why you will accomplish so little and not live the life you were meant to live.

I have had multiple fears that paralyzed me from doing what I was supposed to do in terms of saving money. I was afraid of losing all my money in the stock market overnight, afraid of studying in Germany, and afraid of speaking in public. The list goes on and on.

The previous chapter and this one were the most difficult for me to write, as they reminded me of all the bad choices I made and the fear I had of making any decisions. All of this leads to procrastination. If fears prevent you from moving ahead, follow me further into this chapter, and let us discover together how to use fear to your advantage to become the person you were meant to be. Life is too short to let fear dictate your future. Every outstanding achievement sometimes lies on the right side of your fear. Let's dive in without losing too much time.

Fear

> *"I am lucky that whatever fear I have inside me,*
> *my desire to win is always stronger."*
> **Serena Williams**

How many great ideas did you have in the past six months? How many of them did you try?

Why did you not try them? Because of the fear of failure and maybe the fear of judgment by your closest friends, family, and coworkers. If you have this feeling, don't worry, almost everyone has had it. What we need to understand is that getting a great idea is the easy part of the equation. Getting started and acting is what separates successful people from the rest. Fear of failure is a natural part of life. Nobody, not even me, wants to fail. However, as stated by Serena Williams, the only way to succeed is to have the deep desire inside you to face your fear and to act upon it. Unfortunately, this is the way most people live today, by choosing to play it safe and avoid any possibility of failure. As the Japanese proverb teaches: "Fall seven times, rise eight."

Action to Conquer Your Fear

> "I learned that courage is not the absence of fear, but the triumph over it. The brave man is not he who does not feel afraid, but he who conquers that fear."
> **Nelson Mandela**

It takes willingness, courage, commitment, and grit to accept where you are in life, identify and face your fear, make a plan, and go all in in your transformation process. To conquer any fear, you need to take action. Most of the time when you take action, you will realize that your fears are a bit exaggerated, but you will only see it if you take action.

Throughout my life, I have had so many fears. I had a fear of speaking German in public, in restaurants, or during my time at university. I felt overwhelmed when I had to give a presentation in front of my teammates. Anytime I tried, my fears took over, and I could barely get out a word when it was my turn to speak. I remember my friends telling me that the only way I could conquer this fear was to take action, embrace this challenge, and go out and find every single opportunity to talk to people. The first time I tried, it was very difficult for me to put one word after another. What I realized was that the people were very patient and most of the time helped me find my vocabulary. I kept trying and didn't let my fear paralyze me. I did the same when I decided to write this book. I ignored all naysayers and people's opinions and took action. Don't let your fears stop you from going for your dreams.

Now, let's explore what it means to act by identifying our fears and seeing how we can overcome them by taking action. Below are just a couple of them.

1. Fear of losing your job.

   Action: Work hard, continue showing up, focus on your task, and have regular communication with your boss on how to improve your work. At the end of each Friday, write a summary of your accomplishments and the expectations for the coming week. Don't let fear take total control of your life. Jon Gordon, in his book *The Power of a Positive Team*, said that fear and faith have one thing in common. The first one believes in a positive future while the second one believes in a negative future. So, why let your fear destroy your future? Inside, have faith that your future is bright and keep performing well at work.

2. Fear of delegating.

   Action: Have a discussion with your colleagues and share with them your expectations and timeline. Schedule weekly meetings to check progress, make adjustments where necessary, and let it go (remember to always be a good leader). Don't micromanage; show respect and let them know that you believe in them.

3. Fear of failing a school examination.

   Action: Start studying at the beginning of the lesson and keep going throughout the lesson. As you already know if you follow my work, it is better to work every day and be consistent instead of waiting until the last minute. By doing so, you will remove the fear of failure and get ready for your examination.

4. Fear of making real estate and other investments.
   Action: Identify all the facts (market tendency, interest rates), seek advice *only* from experts (avoid asking advice from people who have never done it before), read books, ask questions, trust your judgment, and act.

5. Fear of things outside your control.
   Action: Remember, the only things you always have total control over are your attitude and your actions. Everything else is beyond your control. The most important thing to remember is to always get back up if something does not go the way you expected. Don't complain, don't blame, and don't find excuses. Keep going and remember that failure is never permanent.

6. Fear of other people's opinions or what they think about you.
   Action: This is one of the greatest fears in our world today. People are so afraid of what other people may say that they miss a lot of opportunities. As stated by Robin Sharma in his book *The Everyday Hero Manifesto*, "Someone's opinion is just someone's opinion." Instead of spending your time and energy on what other people may say, focus on your goal and have the self-discipline to work on it every single day. Each mistake, and failure, brings you closer to your goal. No one achieves their goals without mistakes, and this is why they succeed.

7. Fear of losing all the money you have invested in the stock market.
   Action: Read books on how to invest your money. There are plenty of books out there just waiting to be read. In the Appendix, I will give you a list of the best books I have read on that subject. Making the time to learn and read books on this

subject will help you pick and choose the right investment portfolio based on your level of risk acceptance, and give you a lot of confidence during a bear market.

Don't let fear paralyze you. Be bold and embrace the discomfort that comes with growth. Staying in your comfort zone will only hold you back from pursuing your dreams. To overcome fear and build confidence, take action—right now. Remember, everything you want lies on the other side of fear. Decide what you want and commit to the effort required to achieve it. Nothing happens until you act. Don't just wish and hope—face your fears and take action step by step. The more you act, the more fear will fade. Keep in mind that failure is never permanent. As Winston Churchill said, "Courage is going from failure to failure without losing enthusiasm." Keep pushing forward and believe in yourself. Never give up!

Eliminate Procrastination

"Never put off till tomorrow what you can do today."
Benjamin Franklin

In his book *Hidden Potential*, Adam Grant explains that procrastination isn't a time management problem—it's an emotion management problem. This shift in perspective completely changed how I understood procrastination. Before reading Grant's book, I always felt guilty when I procrastinated and carried that guilt for a long time. His book helped me realize that procrastination often stems from avoiding unpleasant or difficult tasks I didn't want to face. Instead of "eating that frog," I would find reasons to do something more enjoyable.

- Procrastinating by not starting to save money right now and refusing to delay gratification and postponing your saving goal for later will cost you more money in terms of the amount you could have saved if you had started early.
- Procrastinating by not starting to work immediately on your most important task and instead spending your time on low-value activity will cost you more in the long run.
- Procrastinating on your physical fitness will cost you more in terms of your overall health and well-being. Waiting for a better day to start running, waiting for the perfect conditions before buying your gym membership, or convincing yourself that you do not have enough money for a yoga class or a massage will ultimately cost you more.
- Procrastinating by not investing in that online course or buying that book that will help you with the skill you want to acquire will cost you more in terms of your personal development and growth.
- The list goes on...

Looking back, I can easily identify what I have learned from Adan Grant's book. I had found a book that explained to me in detail what I was going through anytime I procrastinated on a task or activity. For example, I had planned to write this book and had the goal to complete it before the end of 2024. I started writing this book at the beginning of the year and stopped after four months and moved to my other goals. It took me one month to remind myself of my *why* and go back to my book. Did I progress during the first four months? Not really.

Why?

Because I kept procrastinating every time I started writing, and knowing that I had other goals that were not so demanding in terms of focus made me automatically switch to those goals. By doing so, I was falling behind on my goals to write and publish my book before the end of this year. I realized that procrastinating in writing my book was also keeping me away from my dream to write and publish this book. I made a plan to write every morning after going through my morning routine, and in the evening after finishing my work and family obligations.

Action Steps

- Automate your repetitive tasks, such as putting money into your savings for retirement or your children's education and paying your bills.
- Always plan your activities the day or week before. Use a calendar or set up a reminder on your phone.
- List your tasks by priority and develop the self-discipline to do the most important one, no matter what, at the planned time.
- Apply the five-minute rule to get motivation and momentum. Keep going after five minutes.
- Remove all distractions until you finish your task.
- Delegate everything you are not good at. For example, if you hate cleaning your house, find out how to pay someone to do it, and use this time to work on yourself.

Check out the Appendix for the list of books that I highly recommend if you want to dig deeper into this subject.

Conclusion

> *"It isn't sufficient just to want. You've got to ask yourself what you are going to do to get the things you want."*
> **Franklin D. Roosevelt**

The difference between successful and unsuccessful people is that the successful ones make a plan, take action, and persist through challenges until they succeed. Unsuccessful people lack written goals, blame others, avoid delayed gratification, and focus on activities that provide immediate pleasure rather than long-term progress. Which group would you choose?

Remember that knowledge without action won't bring success into your life. Only when you use the knowledge you have gained throughout this book and act upon it will you see a positive change in your life. Don't wait until the conditions are perfect and all lights are green; this will never happen. Instead, expect roadblocks, challenges, and difficulties and try to solve them as they arise.

Don't count on luck to help you. Don't let your life and your future pass you by. I don't believe in luck, or I should say I have stopped believing in luck. Since I took back control of my life, I understood that no one would come to save me, no one would ever pay my bills, the economy would never change, inflation would continue to get higher, and taxes would continue to rise. For me, luck is when preparation meets opportunity, period.

Since I started my transformation journey, opportunities have started flowing my way. Some may call it luck, but I know it's the result of hard work. I've seen many people miss out because they're not prepared when opportunities arise. To be ready, work on yourself every day—invest in training, read books, use your commute to learn, attend seminars, seek advice from experts, and always be absorbing knowledge.

Become a value creator. Always be overprepared, communicate well, and listen carefully. Leave everyone better than you found them, give more than expected, and go the extra mile. When new opportunities come, you'll be ready. Go deep in everything you do—refuse to stay at the surface. The deeper you go, the less competition you'll face. Most people stay at the surface, distracted by notifications and scrolling. To stand out, work with focus, intensity, and consistency, block out distractions, and do it for the long haul. Going deeper is key to doing your best work and reducing competition.

The secret to success has always been the same: Anyone willing to do the work can achieve it. The path has already been laid by those who've succeeded before you. By following their example—working hard, being consistent, cultivating good habits, and making smart choices—you too will reach your goals. Nothing can stop you. Use this book as a guide to take action now. Only those who act will see results. To truly transform your life, be prepared to make extraordinary sacrifices. Every great achievement begins with a single step. Keep moving forward, believe in yourself, and never stop pursuing your dreams.

Acknowledgments

My parents (Jacqueline and Daniel B. Djoto)

Thank you for everything you have taught me since I was a child. Your hard work and dedication showed me that anything is possible if you do the work.

My wife (Sandrine N. Djoto)

Thank you for your support throughout this challenging process. Without your support, this book wouldn't be possible. You have always found the right words to keep me motivated.

My sister (Hélène F. Fotso)

Big thanks for helping me become an entrepreneur. You were the first to give me the idea to share my story with the rest of the world. Your encouragement, advice, and support throughout this journey helped me keep going, especially during difficult times. I'm forever grateful for that.

The Many Others

Thank you also to my coach, Scott Allan, best-selling author of *Do the Hard Things First*, for being with me every step of the way and keeping me organized. Your advice has helped me complete this book more than anything else. I'll always be grateful for your support during the entire process.

Thank you to Ashbel Kezi for being there with me from the beginning and encouraging me throughout the process.

Thank you to Arthur Nana, Shane Stapleton, and David Rao. Your friendship and mentorship mean a lot to me. You have always trusted me, and I'm so grateful for that.

And last but not least, thank you to my good friend Abbes Bellil, PhD. You checked weekly on how I was progressing in my book and provided full support and availability to help me move forward. Big thanks.

Appendix

Introduction and Chapter 1. Your Clarity: Your *Why*
1. *Start with Why*, Simon Sinek
2. *Training Camp*, Jon Gordon
3. *Be Bold*, Anna Goldstein
4. *Awaken the Giant Within*, Tony Robbins
5. *Can't Hurt Me*, David Goggins

Chapter 2. Goal Setting
1. *Goals!*, Brian Tracy
2. *The Magic of Thinking Big*, David Schwartz, PhD
3. *The Success Principles*, Jack Canfield
4. *Your Best Year Ever*, Micheal Hyatt
5. *Drive*, Daniel H. Pink

Chapter 3. Improve: Measure and Optimize Your Time Management
1. *Eat that Frog*, Brian Tracy
2. *The Everyday Hero Manifesto*, Robin Sharma
3. *The 4-Hour Workweek*, Timothy Ferriss
4. *Time Wise*, Amantha Imber
5. *The ONE Thing*, Gary Keller and Jay Papasan

Chapter 4. Personal Development
1. *10X is easier than 2X*, Dan Sullivan and Dr. Benjamin Hardy

2. *Grit*, Angela Duckworth
3. *Raise Your Game*, Alan Stein Jr.
4. *The Power of One More*, Ed Mylett
5. *Hidden Potential*, Adam Grant

Chapter 5. Work on Your Fitness and Well-being

1. *Spark*, John Ratey, MD
2. *Why We Sleep*, Matthew Walker, PhD
3. *Eat Smarter*, Shawn Stevenson
4. *Sleep Smarter*, Shawn Stevenson
5. *Change Your Brain Every Day*, Daniel G. Amen, MD

Chapter 6. Develop Your Leadership Skills

1. *The Power of Positive Leadership*, Jon Gordon
2. *Leadership First*, Gifford Thomas
3. *Give and Take*, Adam Grant
4. *Thrive Through the Five*, Dr. Jill M. Siler
5. *The Infinite Game*, Simon Sinek
6. *Uncommon Leadership*, Ben Newman

Chapter 7. Develop Your Communication and Listening Skills

1. *Exactly What to Say*, Phil M. Jones
2. *How to Win Friends and Influence People*, Dale Carnegie
3. *How to Become a People Magnet*, Marc Reklau
4. *How to Talk to Anyone*, Leil Lowndes
5. *The Communication Book*, Mikael Krogerus and Roman Tschäppeler
6. *Speak with Impact*, Allison Shapira
7. *The Fine Art of Small Talk*, Debra Fine
8. *How to Listen*, Oscar Trimboli
9. *InSideOut Coaching*, Joe Ehrmann

Chapter 8. Develop Your Selling Skills
1. *To Sell is Human*, Daniel Pink
2. *The Irresistible Consultant's Guide to Winning Clients*, David A. Fields
3. *People Buy You*, Jeb Blount
4. *The Sales Tightrope*, Katie Mullen
5. *Getting to Yes*, Roger Fisher and William Ury

Chapter 9. Attract, Make, Save, and Invest More Money
1. *The Millionaire Fastlane*, MJ DeMarco
2. *The 10 Pillars of Wealth*, Alex Becker
3. *The Holy Grail of Investing*, Tony Robbins
4. *Rich Dad Poor Dad*, Robert Kiyosaki
5. *The Total Money Makeover*, Dave Ramsey
6. *Multiple Streams of Income*, Robert G. Allen
7. *MONEY Master the Game*, Tony Robbins
8. *The Automatic Millionaire*, David Bach

Chapters 10 and 11. Habits and Routines, and The Power of Your Choices
1. *Atomic Habits*, James Clear
2. *The Power of Habit*, Charles Duhigg
3. *The 5AM Club*, Robin Sharma
4. *The 7 Habits of Highly Effective People*, Stephen R. Covey
5. *The Compound Effect*, Darren Hardy

Chapter 12. Eliminate Fear and Procrastination
1. *Do the Hard Things First*, Scott Allan
2. *Getting Things Done*, David Allen
3. *The War of Art*, Steven Pressfield
4. *The Productivity Project*, Chris Bailey
5. *Deep Work*, Cal Newport

ABOUT THE AUTHOR

Etienne H. Djoto is a senior functional safety engineer based in Ottawa, Canada. His goal is to help people around the world take the next step into a brighter future. When he is not writing on personal development and time management, Djoto can be found reading, traveling, or hiking with his spouse and two daughters. This is his first book. You can find his other writing at medium.com/@herveduva03 or on Facebook and X.

DOWNLOAD YOUR FREE ULTIMATE PRODUCTIVITY PLAYBOOK & TAKE CONTROL OF YOUR LIFE!

READ THIS FIRST

Thank you for investing in You Are the Architect of Your Life! To help you take action and see real results, I'm giving you The Ultimate Productivity Playbook—completely FREE! Inside, you'll discover battle-tested strategies used by top achievers to:

- ✓ Eliminate distractions & stay laser-focused on what truly matters
- ✓ Crush procrastination & take massive action effortlessly
- ✓ Achieve more—without burnout! Learn how to work smarter, not harder
- ✓ Master time management & create unstoppable momentum
- ✓ Boost efficiency with smart habits & daily success rituals
- ✓ And much more…

This is your blueprint for designing a high-performance life!

Don't wait—unlock your full potential now! 👇 Download your FREE copy today! 👇

subscribepage.io/ED_YATAOYL

www.ingramcontent.com/pod-product-compliance
Lightning Source LLC
Chambersburg PA
CBHW071355160426
42811CB00094B/425